When Challenge Brings Change

When Challenge Brings Change

How Teacher Breakthroughs Transform the Classroom

EDITED BY

Sandra Murphy
Mary Ann Smith

Foreword by Elyse Eidman-Aadahl

TEACHERS COLLEGE PRESS

TEACHERS COLLEGE | COLUMBIA UNIVERSITY
NEW YORK AND LONDON

national
writing
project

2120 UNIVERSITY AVE,
BERKELEY, CA 94704

Published simultaneously by Teachers College Press, 1234 Amsterdam Avenue, New York, NY 10027 and National Writing Project, 2120 University Ave, Berkeley, CA 94704.

Through its mission, the National Writing Project (NWP) focuses the knowledge, expertise, and leadership of our nation's educators on sustained efforts to help youth become successful writers and learners. NWP works in partnership with local Writing Project sites, located on nearly 200 university and college campuses, to provide high-quality professional development in schools, universities, libraries, museums, and after-school programs. NWP envisions a future where every person is an accomplished writer, engaged learner, and active participant in a digital, interconnected world.

Front cover design by Edwin Kuo. Illustration by Vitezslav Valka/Shutterstock.

Pages 98–99: Tony Hoagland, excerpts from "Personal" from *Unincorporated Persons in the Late Honda Dynasty*. Copyright © 2010 by Tony Hoagland. Reprinted with the permission of The Permissions Company, LLC on behalf of Graywolf Press, graywolfpress.org.

Library of Congress Cataloging-in-Publication Data

Names: Murphy, Sandra (Sandra M.), editor. | Smith, Mary Ann, 1942– editor.
Title: When challenge brings change : how teacher breakthroughs transform the classroom / Edited by Sandra Murphy and Mary Ann Smith ; Foreword by Elyse Eidman-Aadahl.
Description: New York, NY : Teachers College Press, [2023] | Includes bibliographical references and index. | Summary: "These narratives share teacher breakthroughs-the ways teachers have successfully and courageously turned a corner"—Provided by publisher.
Identifiers: LCCN 2023019145 (print) | LCCN 2023019146 (ebook) | ISBN 9780807769119 (hardcover) | ISBN 9780807769102 (paperback) | ISBN 9780807782095 (ebook)
Subjects: LCSH: Effective teaching. | Teacher-student relationships. | Teacher effectiveness.
Classification: LCC LB1025.3 .W435 2023 (print) | LCC LB1025.3 (ebook) | DDC 371.102—dc23/eng/20230613
LC record available at https://lccn.loc.gov/2023019145
LC ebook record available at https://lccn.loc.gov/2023019146

ISBN 978-0-8077-6910-2 (paper)
ISBN 978-0-8077-6911-9 (hardcover)
ISBN 978-0-8077-8209-5 (ebook)

Printed on acid-free paper
Manufactured in the United States of America

We dedicate this book to teachers everywhere.
The work you do matters beyond measure.

Contents

Foreword

Breakthroughs. In the media, the word attaches to stories of new cancer treatments, cold fusion experiments, space travel—glorious, world-changing technologies. In real life, though, the word points to something simpler, but more profound: the human experience of breaking through some limiting belief to achieve some new, perhaps transformational, understanding.

In this volume, editors Sandra Murphy and Mary Ann Smith have gathered 11 accomplished teachers to tell stories of transformative learning, learning that earns the label "breakthrough." And as a fellow teacher, I'm here for it. Teaching, like parenting, is a long-term proposition that asks us to have faith that a course of action will pay off over time. Of course, we tweak, we modify, we individualize; every student and every class are different. But broad outlines and experienced repertoires remain. It all usually works, until it doesn't.

Reading this wonderful collection, full of insights into effective and sustained teaching, one is reminded again and again of how deeply personal the pursuit of breakthroughs can be and how much can be learned from the shared stories of these journeys. The teachers collected here have all participated in a Bay Area Writing Project program and their journeys reminded me of my own moments of transformational learning.

I remembered a particular occasion when a small group of us at the Maryland Writing Project were sitting around a conference table surrounded by chart paper, sticky notes, and small cassette recorders. It was probably around November, and Pam Morgan, an extraordinary Baltimore City teacher, was venting—again. Like each of us in that small group, she had taken up the challenge of documenting and publishing a successful curricular approach, one for which she was well-known and that she had honed over several years. The stakes were high: Her curriculum inquiry would feed into a larger teacher-led study of what successful teaching looked like in urban classrooms.

Only this year, her students just weren't having it—not one bit.

From September to November, Pam continued on faith, giving it time. Who wouldn't? All of us in the group had been supportive over her several months of wrestling with her class and with herself. But finally one of us, a high school teacher, stopped the conversation to ask in frustration, "So Pam, what *is* working in your classroom this year?"

Things usually work, until they don't. After a startled reaction and a few days of reflection, Pam came to embrace the question: "What *is* working in your classroom?" and to set aside dwelling on a curriculum that ought to work in order to find a new understanding of what did work. When she later wrote about that year in her classroom, her "finely honed curricular approach" had been transformed into an understanding of her students' experience of real audiences and their emerging desire to connect. She titled her piece "All Roads Lead to Roam," and in it, she points to the question as the start of her breakthrough learning.

It was Pam's story, but we all learned from it because she had the courage and tenacity to make it public. What teacher hasn't had some "special thing" that always worked until it didn't? Who hasn't wondered whether to keep going or to pivot to something new? In teaching, don't all roads eventually lead to roam?

Pam's breakthrough was a gift to all of us. And that's what this book is, too. Editors Murphy and Smith nested their invitation to their breakthrough writers within the culture of the Bay Area Writing Project, a culture with roots that go back 50 years to 1974 when a small group of teachers and professors convened a Summer Institute at the University of California, Berkeley. From that first institute, the basic conditions were set for transformational breakthroughs: close examinations of practice presented in public, time and space for questioning and reflection, critical friendship and colleagueship, and writing—lots of writing. Over several years, Bay Area educators refined and expanded the model of the Bay Area Writing Project and, from those roots grew the National Writing Project network.

I owe my memories to the National Writing Project, but in truth, the conditions for transformational learning among teachers—for real breakthroughs—can be found wherever teachers are supported to take up hard questions in a spirit of inquiry and respect for even the most mundane elements of the teachers' craft. It thrives in high-quality professional learning, in professional learning communities and teachers' school improvement networks, and among faculty where supportive camaraderie is mixed with high expectations and gentle accountability. And it benefits, above all, from the practice of writing itself, particularly when done in a community that will react, draft by draft, to the journey unfolding.

I take this book as inspiration that challenges us all to create environments where teachers can pursue the new knowledge and understandings that constitute meaningful breakthroughs. May all roads lead to roam.

Elyse Eidman-Aadahl
Executive Director, National Writing Project

Acknowledgments

With gratitude to the **Bay Area Writing Project** (BAWP) for supporting the breakthroughs project and for 50 years of giving voice to teachers wherever they are in their teaching lives.

Congratulations to the **National Writing Project** (NWP), celebrating 50 years and counting. Thank you for endorsing the breakthroughs project and for five extraordinary decades of encouraging teachers to tell their stories.

CHAPTER 1

Introduction

Sandra Murphy and Mary Ann Smith

> *Name a breakthrough you experienced in your teaching—a moment of clarity, a kind of reset, a new understanding or approach, or even an epiphany.*
>
> *As you read what follows, think about your own breakthrough and what it might mean to write about it.*

Every teacher—for that matter, every human being—has at some time experienced a breakthrough; whether it's gaining a new insight, solving a problem, making a discovery, or salvaging an almost-lost-cause. The breakthrough can be transformative—a moment when something seems to shift or some corner gets turned, however haltingly. Writing about it adds another dimension of transformation, when writers put themselves in the story and gain a fresh take on what happened.

When breakthroughs crop up in schools and classrooms, they often come about because old rituals have crumbled. What has worked in the past is no longer sustainable. It's time for a change of some kind—whether a measured change, an exhilarating leap forward, or a hard-won new understanding. Often there is a "triggering problem" (Whitney, 2008, p. 157) that leads to the breakthrough—what Jack Mezirow (1991) calls a "disorienting dilemma" (p. 177) that signals something is going wrong.

Teachers are in the unique position of having to respond minute by minute to what is in front of them, a daunting enterprise that demands constant and unrelenting attention. Their daily survival—working with the here and now—often poses limits on their bandwidth to do more, to think transformatively beyond the moment at hand.

Yet even with their everyday classroom demands, teachers manage to consider and act upon ideas for making things better. Several decades ago in 2002, the National Writing Project published a book called *Breakthroughs: Classroom Discoveries About Teaching Writing*. The book featured essays that followed a teacher and writer "on a rocky teaching road that sometimes led to a gradual discovery and sometimes culminated in an aha moment" (Bauman & Peterson, 2002, para 4). Teaching, the book editors claimed, called for an optimistic approach ("Hey, I can do this.") to solving puzzles (Bauman & Peterson, 2002, p. 2).

The editors intended to show that accomplished teachers "know that it must be their mission, and that of their creative colleagues, to invent better classrooms" (Bauman & Peterson, 2002, p. 2). The teachers who were represented in the original *Breakthroughs* book embraced the idea that "they and their students need to be on the front line of educational solutions" (p. 2).

When we reread the original *Breakthroughs* book, it occurred to us that the very act of writing about breakthroughs could be transformative—a process of revisiting, and perhaps reseeing, an event or series of events, a long-standing question, or a moment of truth. As Ershler (2001) describes it, "the narrative process affords teachers the opportunity to see themselves in the stories they tell" (p. 169). If teaching is an act of optimism, so can writing be a positive act, a new breath of air, a view from a different angle.

And so, with the support of the Bay Area Writing Project, we began what we called "The BAWP Breakthroughs Project" with an invitation to teachers to write their stories and perhaps to find out something they might not have realized before. (For a step-by-step plan of the project, see tcpress.com/challenge-appendix.) Our starting point sounded something like this: "We want your story, told and interpreted by you, for the purpose of sharing your discoveries and insights with other teachers." We had some initial questions in mind, especially after reading about breakthroughs that occurred two decades ago:

- What do we mean by the idea of a breakthrough, and what does a breakthrough look like in this decade?
- To what extent might a breakthrough be transformative? In other words, when does a breakthrough go beyond something incremental or makeshift and become something that actually changes a mind or upends a way of doing things?
- Does writing about a breakthrough enhance its transformative power?

ABOUT THIS COLLECTION

In this collection, 11 teachers describe the process of transforming their teaching in some way—to meet the demands of the moment, as well as demands that may have haunted them for years. The collection illustrates how these teachers use their breakthroughs to come up with fresh ways of thinking and of interacting with students.

You might notice that the narrative structure of each story is different. Some are chronological, some vignettes, some episodic. Regardless of structure, the stories are infused with humor, confessions, reflections, and moments of drama. And in every case they are told with a strong, unique narrative voice.

Not all the breakthroughs here are the same by any means. They range from stories about changes in curriculum and practice to stories about personal identity in the classroom. What motivates each breakthrough also varies widely. Some emerge from a teacher's own reading or writing experience, some from an urgent school or classroom necessity, and some from events outside of school. They reveal what is often untold about the teaching life— what keeps teachers going, the challenges they face, the beliefs they live by, and the commitment and empathy they bring to their students. In sum, the breakthroughs represent the richness, complexity, and indefiniteness, even precariousness, of a teacher's experience.

The stories, then, differ one from another, but they have four themes in common which we describe here, along with why these are significant.

- *Care and concern for students*: for their well-being, for what and how they learn, for giving them authority, for connecting with their lives and circumstances, with their interests and aspirations, and for what will help them succeed.
- *Exploration of self-doubt, self-discovery, and those questions that just don't go away*: The importance of looking into things and especially of writing about explorations cannot be overestimated. While we can't observe the daily reflection teachers do, when it is made visible as it is in this collection, "the profession garners a new respect for the complexity teaching entails" (Dana, 2002, para 6).
- *Breaking rules and taking risks*: Where would we be without the courage of teachers to recognize the need for change and act on it? Courageous teachers are willing to "challenge mainstream knowledge and conventional wisdom" (Nieto, 2006, p. 457). They are also flexible, meaning they are "prepared for uncertainty" (p. 468) and for making the most of it.
- *Personal identity*: Who we are in the classroom, how we choose to share ourselves, matters mightily. Parker Palmer (2017) defines personal identity as "a moving intersection" of inner forces such as our genetic makeup, outer forces such as the culture in which we were raised, and the people and experiences that have helped shape us (p. 14). According to Palmer, good teachers have one trait in common: "a strong sense of personal identity infuses their work" (p. 11).

In addition to the themes, each breakthrough in this collection brings alive an evolution of some kind—whether an invention, a reformulation, or a different way of thinking—and embedded in each are practical takeaways. You will see specific readings and assignments that may be useful in your classrooms. That said, the takeaways in this book are intended for inspiration, not imitation. The emphasis here is not on the latest platform or the ultimate lesson plan. It's on how we stare down the challenges in teaching that work away at us, that nudge us to break through whatever is standing in the way of making things better.

The teachers in this collection work with older students. While their stories are situated in high school, community college, and college class-rooms, the insights and ideas they present are applicable to other grade levels. Collectively they show the side of teaching that is too often hidden from view—the detours and discomforts, and yes, also the joy. The break-through stories go to the best source for an authentic view of teaching as it really happens—teachers paying attention to the signals, the nuances, and the moments of truth, and then making something of them.

THE ROLE OF REFLECTION AND REFRAMING IN BREAKTHROUGHS

When we began working with teachers on the idea of writing about their breakthroughs, we were casting a net, hoping to catch what goes on in the minds of teachers when they are facing a challenge or a pressing issue, and to find out what happens then: what change looks like for them and for their students. We hoped to shine a light on any reflections that might come up. Reflective teachers, according to Zeichner (2005), enter the stage as impor-tant contributors to the field's knowledge—a field traditionally seen as "the exclusive property of colleges, universities, and research and development centres" (p. 10).

Zeichner (2005) claims that all teachers are reflective in some way, but it's the kind of reflection, what exactly teachers are reflecting on, and most significant to us "how they are going about it" (p. 18) that matters. While engaging in thoughtful reflection is important to improving practice, some-where in the mix, it seemed to us, teachers themselves must undergo some kind of internal shift so as to reorder their classroom world.

Here is where transformation comes in and where we turn to the work of Anne Elrod Whitney (2008) who describes what it means to experience a transformative change as a teacher. In her study of seven teachers in one National Writing Project (NWP) Summer Institute, Whitney observes the kinds of changes teachers make in their thinking— the reframing they do to understand and respond to challenges they en-counter in their work.

This idea of reframing is key to transformations or breakthroughs. We have to shed our old looking glass for an all-new set of lenses: "Normally, when we learn something, we attribute an old meaning to a new experience. In transformative learning, however, we reinterpret an old experience or a new one from a new set of expectations" (Mezirow, 1991, p. 11).

Whitney examines how these shifts in expectations come about dur-ing NWP institutes where teachers have the support of their colleagues and opportunities to write. She then looks at the kinds of transformations that come about as a result. She notes the power of reframing for teachers as it brought about "a new sense of authority and, therefore, opened up not only new ways of seeing but also new ways of being" (p. 168).

WRITING AS A WAY TO PROMOTE TRANSFORMATIONAL LEARNING

Whitney describes how writing can promote self-reflection and ultimately, transformation. One of the participants in Whitney's (2008) study of the Summer Institute, Liz, describes her self-examination through writing as "like finding a secret door in my house" (p. 162). Through writing, Liz comes upon "thoughts, feelings, and opinions (things she termed 'epiphanies') that she had not been aware she held—or at least she had not been aware she held so deeply" (p. 162).

Historically, other scholars have weighed in on the importance of writing as a tool for thinking, exploring, and reflecting. The British scholar James Britton (1970) promoted the idea of using expressive language, "written language favourable to discovery and learning," to make sense of our experience (p. 291). It was an idea that made its way across the ocean and caught on here in the United States.

A few years later, in her landmark article, "Writing as a Mode of Learning," Janet Emig (1977) proposed the idea that writing represents a unique form of learning because it actively integrates process and product and voila! You can see writing unfold, think about it, be propelled by it, and tweak it. In other words, you can learn as you go. In terms of writing as a transformational activity, the writing process encourages reframing.

Writing to learn also became part of popular literature. William Zinsser (1988), an American journalist and literary critic, went on his own writing journey to discover that:

> Writing enables us to find out what we know—and what we don't know—about whatever we're trying to learn. Putting an idea into written words is like defrosting the windshield: The idea, so vague out there in the murk, slowly begins to gather itself into a sensible shape. (p. 16)

More recently, there has been a renewed emphasis on daily writing to promote creative thinking—an idea that is very much alive in popular culture. In her book *The Artist's Way*, Julia Cameron (2016) calls for "morning pages," three pages of stream of consciousness writing done first thing in the morning, in which "nothing is too petty, too silly, too stupid" (p. 10). The theory here is that the uncensored flow of words will tap into thoughts that are lurking below the surface, shut off any internal critics, and bring forth our creative insights.

A word here about narrative writing—the story writing we asked of the breakthrough authors. Diamond (1993) notes that "fuller realization of individual intention and even transformation of perspective can be accomplished through the uses of narrative" (p. 512). Elbow (1986), too, praises narrative as a means to open up personal knowledge, resulting in our "wandering into insights" (as quoted in Diamond, 1993, p. 512).

Writing does not have to be an isolated activity. In her study of the Summer Institute, Whitney (2008) cites the power of sharing writing with a group of peers. For example, after feedback from the group, Laura felt encouraged to continue her piece "expanding and revising it for a public reading" (p. 159). The group operated "by being positive cheerleaders who said, 'You can do it,' but more specifically as mirrors in which Laura had the opportunity to see her own writing from another person's perspective" (p. 159).

Teacher and writer Christine M. Dawson (2017) notes that writing is often "portrayed as a solitary act, conjuring images of an individual bent over a computer keyboard or notebook. It may be hard to get excited about that kind of writing, especially after a long day of teaching!" (p. 3). Like Whitney, Dawson describes the power of sharing writing with others, emphasizing the benefit of having multiple responses and interpretations. "Thus, as teacher-writers invent text, they are also, in a way, inventing and *being invented*, by themselves and others, within the social context of writing group meetings" (p. 4).

We might note here that our breakthroughs authors participated in several group settings designed to encourage their writing, although these were limited to Zoom because of the pandemic. The writing groups dished out much-needed motivation at a time when all of us were feeling isolated. As tired as teachers were at the end of the day, they tuned in for the companionship and collegiality that comes about when writers share their work. Like the teachers in Whitney's study, the breakthroughs authors experienced the gamut of response—from the simple "keep going" kind of response to "more substantive (and riskier) responses that would help them to revise the writing" (2008, p. 160).

Even within the limits of Zoom, we noted that teachers gained additional confidence and authority when they shared their ideas and writing with colleagues. For although teachers can speak and write authentically about what happens in their classrooms, they benefit greatly from the validation and mutual understanding of their peers. The writing group, then, plays a central role in helping its members write with assurance as the experts of their own lived experience.

Finally, Whitney observes that writing is a step toward reframing particular stances, a phenomenon that has practical applications as well. We know of a group of teachers who began every faculty meeting with writing and used writing to address campus problems together. Whether in faculty or department meetings, writing groups, other group settings, or with writing buddies, the writing we do has the potential to get to the very bottom of things.

AUTHORS COMMENT ON THE TRANSFORMATIVE POWER OF WRITING

As for the transformative power of writing about their breakthroughs, the authors offer several views. Kelly Crosby of University of California Davis revised her story at least a dozen times—adding, subtracting, and scrubbing. Each revision, however small, brought up new thoughts and questions for her. We asked her about her experience. Did the writing itself have any effect on her and if so, how might she describe it to another teacher? Her answer:

> I'd never written formally about my teaching until this piece. . . . If you're like me, you can think of all the reasons why your writing (the inherently social action we know so well) may not be ready for a wider audience. This hesitation took me through many drafts of my piece, but with each new take on my writing came a new way of thinking about my teaching, my students, and our collective identity as writers. Writing about your breakthrough? Highly recommended. Five stars. (Personal communication, June 3, 2022)

John Levine at University of California Berkeley actually started out with the notion that the writing was going to tell him something he didn't already know. He explains:

> We give our students writing assignments; that's what we do. But how often do we give ourselves assignments? In writing this piece about my students from three and four years ago, I gave myself the assignment to find out where they landed and how what they learned in my class affected them. I then could compare what I thought I was teaching them and what they actually took away from the class. The results were surprising! (Personal communication, June 4, 2022)

In both of these instances, writing serves as a pathway to discovery, to what Crosby calls "a new way of thinking."

For James Wilson, writing has brought his identity and self-worth into sharp focus:

> As I have gotten older, I have increasingly relied on writing to figure myself out: in reflecting and crafting a story about myself, I bring that self into being. This was especially true with this breakthrough piece, in which I traced my own developing sense of myself as a teacher. In practice, that evolution often feels

tentative and unfinished to me, but writing this piece has helped me see my own story better and gives me the confidence to become the teacher and the person I want to be. (Personal communication, June 13, 2022)

While the act of writing may add extra layers of insight, discovery, or recognition to a lived experience like a breakthrough, one of our authors sees the mere decision to write as the centerpiece. In her chapter, Cheryl Hogue Smith brings to life her own up-and-down writing journey, the moments of pain it caused her and the fact that she wanted to save her students from the same pain.

While my story explains the breakthroughs I had with my relationship with writing and the pedagogical choices I made so my students could experience the same kind of breakthrough, in a move I can only describe as "breakthrough therapy," the more profound breakthrough may very well have been that I wrote about it at all. (Personal communication, June 6, 2022)

These testimonies to the transformative power of writing set the stage for what's to come: stories about what is real and true for 11 veteran teachers as they revisit their experiences through the gift of writing. We hope their stories motivate and inspire you to write about your own challenges and breakthroughs, and as Yrsa Daley-Ward (2021) encourages us, bring them "into the present with new eyes, today's eyes . . . allow them to bloom, to have their say" (p. 119).

About Chapter 2

Community college teacher **Cheryl Hogue Smith** knows firsthand what it means to be on the receiving end of discouraging comments. Criticized by her dissertation advisor and later rejected by peer reviewers during her first attempt at publishing, she thinks of herself as a "basic writer." To make a comeback, Smith gives her next efforts a shot of technology and a dose of *wyrd*, thereby pushing the boundaries of what counts as academic writing.

As she turns the tide, replacing rejection with success, Smith uses her newfound discoveries to boost the confidence and courage of the struggling writers in her classroom who have had their own negative experiences with writing. She shares with us assignments and the student work they produce to illustrate "victories that lead to the fun and joy of writing."

CHAPTER 2

Breaking Through Writing Anxiety

Confessions of a Recovering Basic Writer

Cheryl Hogue Smith

My name is Cheryl, and I am a basic writer. I didn't know this, really, until my former dissertation director constantly pointed out what he would call my "infelicitous prose" and ridiculed me for not noticing myself when my thinking was breaking down on the page. The irony that my dissertation was about basic writers didn't escape him, which he was all too happy to point out.[1]

I have most often taught struggling students throughout my teaching career; the last fifteen years have been at a large urban community college. My scholarship mainly focuses on struggling readers and writers—most recently those in first-year composition—and explores ways to help them change the way they view the act of reading, manage the difficult thoughts they are grappling with, and clarify their thinking through their writing. I frequently speak about their fear of failure and their fear of being "wrong," which I, as well as countless other scholars, believe hinders their academic performance (Cox, 2009; De Castella et al., 2013; Rose, 1989; & Smith 2012, for example). But perhaps what I should be writing about is *why* their fear of failure and of being wrong is so scary, *why* it can shut them down. Because who better to explain this than a fellow basic writer who understands well that being perceived as "stupid" paralyzes us with fear?

I'll never forget the day I decided to quit my Ph.D. program and give up on the degree. For months, I had been receiving insensitive criticism on my dissertation from my advisor, and I couldn't understand why he was being so callous in his remarks. I was sending *rough* draft chapters, asking in an accompanying email for help with identifying the parts where my thinking was unclear. However, I discovered much later that he read my chapters closely as though I was submitting *final* drafts, and here's just a smattering of what I received back: "Your most infelicitous sentences are merely the result of hasty inattentive composition and have much more to do with the fact that you are writing too fast and may have a tin ear sometimes for academic prose"; and, "You sometimes look like a basic writer or basic reader in the prose of this chapter, because you are a relatively inexperienced participant in the discourse that this chapter participates in"; and "Is that English? It's like Martian"; and "This is a scholarly document, not a post-card from the beach." Each chapter was saturated with such comments that told me I was obviously in over my head. I could see, after all, that he wasn't wrong in his criticism because after he pointed out a problem, I immediately understood what he was talking about. And throughout this process, chapter after chapter, I became convinced that his comments could only mean that I was stupid.

So I quit.

Okay, I didn't quit for very long because I did somehow manage to work through my ideas and finish the dissertation. But really: Would it have been so difficult for my advisor to say, "I am not sure what you mean here in relation to the last part," instead of "You sometimes look like a basic writer or basic reader in the prose of this chapter"? I cannot begin to describe the irreparable damage my dissertation director caused me.

I tell my story not because I think it's profound in any way, but because it sets up the rest of the story about how I learned to neutralize—or, at least, to manage—the fear that often consumed me as I wrote; I also learned how to use my experiences to help my students work through some of their own struggles with writing.

LEANING INTO THE WYRD

I have had some success with writing, but I struggle with the identity of "writer"—in part because writing has been excruciating for me. However, I recently realized, to my utter surprise, that even though it was still chal-lenging, somewhere along the way, writing also became . . . dare I say . . . fun? When I grasped that I had made a massive shift with my relationship with writing, I knew I had to discover how and why it happened so I could try to replicate that shift for my struggling students, of which there were many, even in first-year composition. After all, if I, a self-professed basic writer, could productively deal with the pain of ridicule and the fear of failure that lies deep within me, then so could they. And as someone who'd been through it, I was well-situated to help them navigate the process. So I traced that shift back and now recognize it occurred when I began bucking the traditional norms of professional academic writing. I was having fun, I realized, because I was leaning into the wyrd.

The earliest meaning of "weird" or "wyrd" was "having the power to control destiny" (Weird Etymology, 2021). Certainly, I felt I had neither "power" nor "control" while I was writing my dissertation—only a wing and a prayer that I could successfully finish. In my postdissertation writ-ing I continued to avoid the "wyrd." But then it was because I had relin-quished my "power" to those whom I thought would "control my destiny":

the gatekeepers, otherwise known as the reviewers of academic journals (Larson, 2018, p. 128). When I was writing to them, I was writing in ways I can only describe as, borrowing from Bartholomae, "inventing the academic journal." That is, I tried "to appropriate (or be appropriated by) a specialized discourse," and in doing so I often felt that the writing had "come *through*" me, not "from" me (Bartholomae, 1985, pp. 135, 138, author's emphasis). I wrote in ways meant to sound like I knew what I was doing, ways that came unnaturally to me. I was like the student Bartholomae describes who wrote "tidy, pat discourse" that sacrificed "creativity" (1985, p. 162). My writing was grammatically correct, but it was also boring and, apparently, infelicitous. And it was far from wyrd.

The first time I submitted an article, it received a "revise and resubmit"; it was then rejected for the very changes the reviewers asked me to make. I didn't write again for years, and that article remains buried somewhere in an old computer. My second attempt at publishing fared only slightly better: I submitted and again received a "revise and resubmit," but I disagreed so vehemently with the direction the editor and reviewers wanted me to take the article that I withdrew the manuscript and sat on it for years. Pasi Ahonen et al. (2020) sum up perfectly how I felt about writing when I was trying to conform to the rules set forth by academic journals: "Writing becomes fragmented, flat, disembodied, and it lacks depth," which, in turn, can make writers "cynical and angry" and make them want to "resist" conforming to that kind of writing (p. 459). I wouldn't necessarily argue that my writing lacked the depth Ahonen et al. describe, but it certainly betrayed the fact that I felt no joy in writing and wanted to resist doing it.[2]

The truth is that publishing is a difficult and sometimes disheartening experience (Ahonen et al., 2020; Kiriakos & Tienari, 2018; Larson, 2018), but it is also a vital experience that two-year college instructors need to go through if we ever want our voices to be heard (Andelora, 2008; Jensen et al., 2021; Sullivan, 2015a; Toth et al., 2019). Even though our workloads are high, and our students deserve much of our attention, we must find the time to put those voices out there (Larson, 2018). This is a scary prospect for even the most accomplished writers, let alone those writers like me, who struggle with language and fear of failure.

As Cassandra Phillips and Joanne Baird Giordano (2020) point out, failure with academic journals is part of a scholar's life, but we learn to forge ahead and try again (p. 157). To that end, I eventually did publish, finding entrée through my use of highly idiosyncratic yet conceptually apt analogies having to do with gorillas and with my years of experience as a scuba diver. However, I still didn't find much pleasure in writing these articles. Yet I did manage to get them published, and I continued to publish—mostly because I work in a university system that requires all of its two-year tenure-track faculty to publish. But perhaps it's also because, as Ahonen et al. (2020) argue, publishing in "academia can be an addictive, fascinating place if one can develop a somewhat functional existence in it" (p. 458). Given my experiences as outlined above, I was surprised I had developed my own "functional existence" within the academic publishing world, but truth be told, I think I was able to do so largely because my former dissertation director continually nagged me to pursue my ideas beyond my dissertation. Therefore, while I did quit—for a day—because of him, I also published because he helped me believe that my ideas had worth and needed to be heard. So I did come to recognize that I had something to say, that I *could* contribute to the field through my writing.

On TikTok, a video showing a moving mechanical horse is making the rounds. It tells viewers, "If you see the horse walking forward, you're left brained (analytical, logical). If you see it walking backward, you're right-brained (creative, intuitive)." A few years ago, I took a similar "test" and was surprised to have it tell me I was more creative than logical. (And yes; the horse *is* moving backwards.) Of course, these tests are silly, but the "results" did get me thinking: Was my own resistance to writing in part because I was so concerned with the logic of an argument and the academic norms I felt I had to follow that I, like the student Bartholomae described, sacrificed creativity?

I have come to realize over the years how creative my community college students are, and their creativity might explain, at least in part, their hostility to the academic work they experienced in high school. Since traditional assignments seemed to suck the life out of most of my students, I tapped into their creativity by incorporating into my first-year composition class a multimodal assignment that asked students to combine texts, images, and music into a video. Predictably, students did well on the multimodal assignment, and, for many, that success helped them to succeed on subsequent, more traditional assignments. (For more about this assignment and their success, see Smith, 2019.) Could the same type of success happen for me? I had always wanted to write about my students' experiences with that multimodal assignment, but I struggled to figure out how to even begin. Then, one day, I had an epiphany: I needed to create a multimodal "article" that would help "readers" *experience* the project on the meta level of a multimodal article about a multimodal assignment. So, when Holly Hassel, former editor of *Teaching English in the Two-Year College*, gave me the go-ahead to try, I embraced the wyrd and used my power to control my destiny by creating a scholarly video. And I had fun drafting it because the challenge and freedom of creating such an article fed my soul. Much to my surprise, the reviewers provided particularly encouraging and generous feedback for this very wyrd endeavor.

Most recently, I struggled with writing an article about six years' worth of student data that explored why students were successfully executing final papers about a book they had not read. It wasn't until I decided to couch the entire piece within a 1959 episode of *The Twilight Zone* that the article came together—and came together quickly. Once again, the reviews were positive, and, once again, I enjoyed the experience of writing it. Who was I, and what had I done with the struggling writer with the tin ear for academic prose? And how could I mimic my creative experiences and successes for my students—students who themselves had been beaten down for their writing—so that more of them could have the same transformation with their relationship with writing as I had?

CREATIVE FREEDOM IN FIRST-YEAR COMPOSITION

Obviously, I am not the first person to talk about creativity in the classroom. Patrick Sullivan argues that students should be both critical and creative thinkers. To that end, teachers need to foster creativity with assignments that circumvent the kinds of perfunctory writing that derive from instruction that focuses on sentence-level error and five-paragraph formats that yield clichéd, surface-level thinking (Sullivan, 2015b, p. 29). In addition, many community college students have regularly been told they are not strong writers, often because their writing doesn't conform to racially unjust notions of what language should be or look like. It's not difficult to see that their past academic experiences led to counterproductive reading and writing habits that work against their success as students (Smith, 2019). Sadly, some students learn that if they put little of themselves into their work they can attribute any failure "to lack of effort rather than lack of ability" (De Castella et al., 2013, p. 864). I understand well what it feels like to want to just get through a task. I see now that, while I wasn't always bold enough to ask an editor if I could do something completely wyrd like create a video for a print journal, I was, in my own small way, trying to grab control of my writing destiny because I always did include something a little wyrd, like scuba diving riddles and inconspicuous gorillas, to begin any article. But that little bit of wyrdness caused me to form an attachment to those pieces of writing. Our students often don't have that attachment—or want that attachment if it means they'll experience failure for something they care about. So using my understanding of their fears and successes, and understanding well that creativity can give students a freedom beyond traditional academic norms, I decided to convert a second traditional academic assignment into a multimodal project. Doing so meant that two of my three assignments were now going to tap into the students' creativity. With any luck, the two assignments combined would help students see themselves as strong and capable thinkers and writers.

I should explain that I teach in Brooklyn at a large and diverse community college, in a Learning Communities Program whereby my first-year composition course is linked with an art history survey course taught by a different instructor. My students are taking first-year composition in their first semester. They are full-time students often working full-time or at least several hours part-time, usually traveling on public transportation to and from school for 1 to 2 hours each way. Many also have extensive family obligations, are food and/or housing insecure, and often deal with life circumstances that understandably interfere with or take precedence over their learning. Most of my students have personal interests in the arts—like drawing, music, fashion design, and film/photography—even though their majors are typically in "safe" fields like nursing, business, or criminal justice. My overarching theme in the course is "protest art," and the first assignment asks students to find a piece of art online and discuss how it could be seen as both protest art and propaganda (in a deceptive way), depending on who is looking at it. The final, third project asks students to create a video using images, music, and text to teach their audience about one artist's contributions to the art world and that artist's efforts to make the world a more equitable and just place. To prepare students for this third project, I converted the second assignment from a traditional argument essay to a one-page 8½-by-11-inch flyer that identified the most important information about the work and contributions of one visual artist. To complete this one-page project, I instructed students to do the following:

- Include images of artwork.
- Divide the flyer into sections with headings that represent a distinct topic or category; include relevant background information about the artist, the artist's medium, the importance of the work of the artist to any protest movements, and the influence the artist has had on other artists or on the art world at large.
- Use at least three different sources in each heading or section.
- Limit direct quotations to no more than half of the information.
- Use in total at least five sources.

I thought that the limit of one page would challenge students to become discriminating about how many categories or headings they would create and what kind of information they would need to include or exclude in each. They also would have to be economical and thoughtful in constructing each section, avoiding repetitive or superfluous, or irrelevant information, while taking care to consult multiple sources for accuracy and adequacy in reporting. In addition, I never grade students on language, and I hoped the nontraditional nature of this assignment would help those students who had learned to fixate on their errors to value their voices and learn to develop those voices without fear.

Figure 2.1 shows a sample flyer that is visually representative of what I received.[3] (For color versions of four student flyers, plus my sample, please visit https://tinyurl.com/wyrdflyers.)

Despite the constraints I imposed on the assignment, students had the freedom to design their flyer in whatever way they wanted. I provided no rules about

Figure 2.1. "Mason," Unit 2

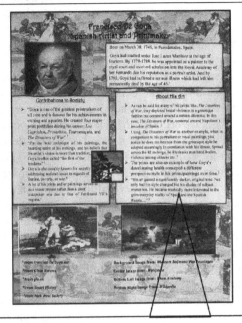

Sample Text, "About His Art"

❖ As can be said for many of his prints like, *The Disasters of War*, they depicted brutal violence in a grotesque fashion but centered around a certain dilemma. In this case, *The Disasters of War*, centered around the Napoleon invasion of Spain. [1]

❖ Using, *The Disasters of War* as another example, when in comparison to his portraiture or royal paintings, you notice he does not hesitate from the grotesque style he adopted assumingly in correlation with his illness. Spread across the 82 etchings, he illustrates mutilated bodies, violence among citizens etc. [5]

❖ The prints are also an example of how Goya's deteriorating health conveyed a different perspective/style in his prints/paintings over time. [2]

❖ "His art gained a significantly darker, original tone. Not only had his style changed but his choice of subject matter too. He became markedly more interested in the grim everyday reality of Spain and the Spanish People..." [3]

font, citation style (although they did need to include a separate Works Cited), color, margins, and so on. Nor again did I grade on language. I was amazed with the final drafts. The flyer format seemed to help students become more adept at paraphrasing and summarizing. In the end, the flyers were beautiful, informative, thorough, and showed evidence of having been created with joy.

Moreover, the categories or topics they developed seemed to help them organize information for the Unit 3 narrative, which essentially took the Unit 2 flyer and converted the categorical information into a multimodal platform (e.g. PowerPoint, iMovie, Presi) using narrative prose. Unsurprisingly, most Unit 3 narratives seemed logically developed, well-informed, and reasonably comprehensive. The flyer assignment seemed to help students understand what it means to *synthesize* multiple sources; instead of writing one paragraph with several main ideas that used a single source—which is what I typically received when I required students to use multiple sources—the paragraphs of their Unit 3 narratives tended to focus on one main idea fleshed out with information drawn from multiple sources, as "Mason's" Unit 3 paragraph demonstrates in Figure 2.2.

In an end-of-semester reflection, I asked students about their experiences with the flyer. The most typical responses I received were from students like "Lilac," who stated, "I had a fun time learning how to use Google Slides to create a flyer format. I also enjoyed reading articles and looking at the artist's paintings." Several remarked about the challenges of the assignment, like "Belle," who said, "The flyer seemed a little intimidating at first because I have never done something like that or close to that. . . . Using multiple sources for one category got a little bit tough at certain points because a lot of the sources are saying the same thing, some are just saying it better than others. A lot of trial and error was also involved in order to figure out what sounded best." But most students, when I asked if they would have preferred a traditional

Figure 2.2. Mason, Unit 3

> By 1786, Goya was appointed as a painter to Charles III, king of Spain. Which followed up in him being appointed as a court painter in 1789. Goya not only painted frescoes but was popularly known for his portrait paintings off the influence from a fellow old Master of Art, Rembrandt. The image to the left is known as, *Charles IV of Spain and His Family* is an example of how he illustrated his portraits. However, this was but a turning point in Goya's life and as important, in his art ("Biography"). By 1792, Goya was struck with a mysterious illness that had left him deaf. And as Robert Maclean from the University of Glasgow suggested, many have suspected it was in due to syphilis or polio, however it was inevitable in reverting its result. Whilst many are fairly acquainted with Goya's paintings and portraits, he had also created multiple sets of prints. Some suspected it was in attribute to his illness, his mental distress from the Peninsular War, and even society itself. One of those series of etchings created was known as *Los Caprichos*. . . . Khan Academy's article written by Sarah C. Schaefer covered the famous print and elaborated that the animals depicted in the print are commonly associated as mystery and evil in Spanish folk tradition. Schaefer further emphasizes in Goya's use of the caption of "the sleep of reason" referring that when reason is renounced or tossed away, it results in creating a monster. The print also perfectly exemplifies his use of his newly adopted grotesque style in which transitioned to another series of prints that pushes it much further.

academic assignment over the flyer, admitted that, even though it was difficult, they still preferred the flyer. "Kam," for example, said "I would prefer the project because it opens more creativity in your mind and helps with a lot of thinking and helps learn more about someone." And "J," who emphatically replied, "ABSOLUTELY NOT!"—a sentiment all but one student in three semesters agreed with. In the end, some of the best work I've seen in any first-year composition class has come from those flyers; I could see evidence of actual *thinking* in the way they categorized and included relevant information.

Shane Wood recently interviewed me for the *Pedagogue* podcast and asked about my goals for first-year composition. In part, I said I wanted students to recognize that if they have trouble understanding a text, it's likely a measure of the difficulty of the text; that confusion and frustration are part of the reading and writing processes; that their interpretations of texts are valued and important; and that they are capable of doing whatever they put their minds to, when often they've been told otherwise. Mostly, however, I wanted to find ways to help those who fear failure shed that fear by understanding that failure is part of the process. To do that, I knew students had to first experience victories so they could know how it feels to succeed ("Episode," 2021). And the flyer and narrative projects are major victories for students because students can write with a confidence that I hope they carry with them after they leave my class and use the skills they learned when faced with more traditional academic assignments.

I confess I was worried that the flyer would be too easy, yet I intuitively felt it was going to be challenging and engaging. I needn't have worried; they found the assignment difficult to execute. I can't ignore, however, that in the same breath, most expressed how much they enjoyed the process of creating the flyer. "Amanda" for example, admits, "I really enjoyed doing the flier assignment. . . . Doing this assignment is a great way to learn about a certain topic." And J, who said, "I had fun while doing it, it gave me the chance to exercise my creativity." As teachers, we talk often of how we want students to focus on the process instead of the product, and this is one of the most notable times in my teaching memory when students so explicitly spoke of enjoying the *process* of putting an assignment together. As "Marc" said, "doing the flyer" asked them to "really step out the box." They remarked in class how their friends in other classes and schools were writing "boring" papers, while they got to do something "weird." It's the wyrd they were embracing.

CONFESSIONS OF A RECOVERING BASIC WRITER

One fact I can't ignore about my earlier professional writing is that I was holding tight to what I perceived as academic norms. As soon as I took control of my destiny and wrote in the wyrd ways I wanted to write, reviewers became more accepting of my writing. But that's not because I somehow miraculously opened reviewers' eyes and helped them see the light (cue Johnny Cash) and value all things wyrd; they already did. The truth is that I really was "inventing the academic journal" a la Bartholomae (1985) because I was so convinced that my own writing was not good enough. In actuality, most academics want to find love and joy with writing and therefore pursue "alternative forms of writing—even if published in 'scholarly' journals—that speak to the reader and engage with their experience" (Kiriakos & Tienari, 2018, p. 266), although some journals can be, as Ahonen et al. (2020) proclaimed, as rigid and scary as I perceived them to be. But I was able to find love and joy in my writing when I leaned into the wyrd, and by embracing and teaching the wyrd, I helped students find love and joy in their writing. As I said to Shane Wood, once students experience the victories, they will know what it feels like to succeed, and those feelings of success will help them better maneuver through future writing processes that might be, at times, frustrating, fearful, or burdened by unreasonable requirements.

I admit that some of my colleagues don't understand why so much of my course is multimodal and non-traditional, but I imagine that most of my colleagues have never self-identified as a basic writer. And it's that identity that helped me design an assignment that could help my students release some of the emotional baggage they have with writing so that they too could see that the writing process can be joyful and, in their words, "fun" (Lilac, "Paul," J, Marc, Amanda, et al.). I hope they will continue to push through the difficulties they encounter in their writing, even when they receive unhelpful or unjust evaluations that have the potential to crush their confidence.

I have to accept that I will always be a recovering basic writer, an identity that, no matter how much joy I have with writing, still lies somewhere beneath the surface. I know I'm just one cruel or inconsiderate comment away from spiraling into those old familiar feelings of stupidity, which is scary to me because I know that I still "have a tin ear sometimes for academic prose." But I've also come to realize that sometimes "waiting for the slap is worse than getting it. Fear is worse than the pain" (Kiriakos & Tienari, 2018, p. 270), something instructors ought to consider. At least now, as I lean into the wyrd, I am not utterly paralyzed by the fear of having someone review my writing; although I still sometimes work to accept some criticism as it is intended—as a measure of the work presented and not of me. With hope, my students and I, together, will figure out how to overcome our deep-seated insecurities as we continue to embrace the wyrd.

CONCLUSION

As difficult as it is to admit, I'm not altogether sorry that I experienced a acute writing anxiety as a student, because my fear of failure and of being seen as "stupid" ultimately gave me insight into the counterproductive behaviors many of my struggling students exhibited—behaviors that interfered with their ability to learn. And it's this insight that helped me create for them a similar breakthrough with writing anxiety that I had already experienced. That said, I must accept the fact that I will always be a recovering basic writer. I still can, and do, experience a writing anxiety when I receive comments that feed my insecurities. But I have learned to discuss that anxiety with others to move beyond the anxiety that numbs me.

Incidentally, in my story about my former dissertation director, the student also became the teacher. We have had many conversations about the comments he made on my dissertation, and because of those conversations, he has learned to be more sensitive and aware in his responses to the writing and thinking of his current students. That's a step in the right direction. I know I'd still hate to be told that my academic work reads like Martians writing postcards from the beach.[4]

RECOMMENDED READING

The New London Group. (1996). A pedagogy of multiliteracies. *Harvard Educational Review*, 66(1), 60–92.

> In one of the early articles about multimodality, The New London Group attempts "to broaden [the] understanding of literacy and literacy teaching and learning to include negotiating a multiplicity of discourses. [They] . . . extend the idea and scope of literacy pedagogy to account for the context of culturally and linguistically diverse and increasingly globalized societies [and] . . . argue that literacy pedagogy now must account for the burgeoning variety of test forms associated with information and multimedia technologies.

Saidy, C. (2018). Beyond words on the page: Using multimodal composing to aid in the transition to first-year writing. *Teaching English in the Two-Year College*, 45(3), 255–273.

> In this article, Saidy reports on a multimodal podcasting unit conducted during a two-week modified summer bridge program for at-risk incoming first-year students. The examples from student work show how teaching a multimodal genre encourages writers to draw from their prior knowledge of standardized genres learned in high school to effectively transition to college composition.

Smith, C. H. (2019). All truly great thoughts are conceived while walking: Academic inclusion through multimodal walkabouts. *Teaching English in the Two-Year College*, 47(1), 18–21.

> In this multimodal article, I argue that community college students are highly creative and demonstrate how students' success on a multimodal assignment can help them succeed on future, more traditional academic writing assignments.

Sullivan, P. (2015). The UnEssay: Making room for creativity in the composition classroom. *College Composition and Communication*, 67(1), 6–34.

In this article, Sullivan argues that students should be both critical and creative thinkers and that teachers need to foster creativity with assignments that will prevent students from producing the kinds of perfunctory writing that derives from instruction focused on sentence-level error and five-paragraph formats yielding clichéd, surface-level thinking.

NOTES

1. Portions of this article first appeared in *California English* (Smith, "Postcards from the Beach," 2013) and are included/adapted with permission.

2. My experiences with my dissertation director don't begin to compare to those experiences of scholars of color whose work is rejected because it doesn't fit what some would call an academic standard. (See, for example, Aja Martinez's *Counterstory* [2020].) I recognize my story will evoke the struggles that scholars of color experience, and, while I stand by those scholars of color as they fight for their voices to be heard and accepted, my story is more about the feelings of inadequacy induced by rejection and fear of failure, not the cause of that rejection and failure.

3. Student names are pseudonyms, and their work is used with their permission through an IRB process. I made no changes to any text or flyers.

4. With appreciation to the National Council of Teachers of English for permission to adapt Chapter 2 from Smith, C. (2022). Leaning into the wyrd: Confessions of a recovering basic writer. *Teaching English in the Two-Year College, 59*(10), 14–23.

About Chapter 3

For years, community college teacher **Anne Kingsley** discouraged her students from using Wikipedia—until she didn't. Her breakthrough comes when she invites students to contribute content to Wikipedia as "real and tangible reading, sculpting, and reporting of research."

In doing so, Kingsley broadens the community of authors who investigate, write about, and add to the interpretation of history—in this case, for millions of Wikipedia readers across the world. She illustrates for us what it means to "help build histories that might otherwise remain silent, forgotten, or underrepresented." In the final analysis, Kingsley tells us that the heart of her project is not Wikipedia, "it is opening a space for students to experiment with their own authority in technological literacies, language, history, and culture." As a practical matter, Kingsley also encourages us to take advantage of participatory online opportunities, and not be put off by the snags of technology.

CHAPTER 3

Taking Research Public
Participatory Communities and Student Authority Through Wikipedia

Anne Kingsley

I love to tell people, "If you are reading the history of the Harlem Renaissance on Wikipedia where names like these appear—Claude McKay, Georgia Douglas Johnson, Countee Cullen, James Weldon Johnson, Nella Larsen, Rudolph Fisher, Alain Locke, The Crisis, Elise Johnson McDougald, Paul Robeson, Cotton Club—there is a good chance you are reading the contributions of community college students."

In 2013, I decided to centralize Wikipedia within my teaching of research to give students a chance to move their writing beyond classroom walls. Rather than carve out space to avoid the open-source platform, I decided to embrace it. I've been doing so ever since.

My shift to Wikipedia occurred through two converging tributaries. The first: I was teaching a college composition and literature course that focused thematically on the Harlem Renaissance. My students and I had stumbled across full digital scans of early volumes of *The Crisis*, the original publication of the National Association for the Advancement of Colored People (NAACP), started in 1910 and edited by W. E. B. Du Bois. The magazine documented the historical, social, and literary happenings of African Americans during the 20th century. Scrolling through the scanned archival pages of the magazine using Google Books allowed students to witness African American history and literature as it unfolded during the Harlem Renaissance. It also allowed them to see how little of that history is documented now. Suddenly, what students discovered in those pages felt bigger than the classroom, certainly bigger than the traditional research paper, and maybe even bigger than us.

The second tributary: a major conversation on open and participatory research was emerging externally. Wikipedia, the world's largest open-source encyclopedia, was calling for more diverse editorship and research content in response to its gender and racial imbalances of both (Ehlers, 2008). Even though "Do not cite Wikipedia" was a common refrain on classroom syllabi and research instruction, especially at the community college, the "edit" button on Wikipedia suddenly presented a compelling entry point for both my students and me to contribute. Not only would their research add to this significant moment in African American history, their contributions would help diversify editorship on Wikipedia.

After several years of this work, the students' contributions are part of living history. Every so often, I like to time travel through my students' writing projects on Wikipedia from years past, to see what edits remain, what has been revised, expanded, even erased. My Wiki.edu dashboard—an interface the non-profit organization built to help college instructors create and manage Wikipedia projects—gives me a chance to reflect on student work. Each time a project like ours is created, the dashboard catalogs a series of statistics that show how many articles were created, edited, total edits, words added, and total number of views of the articles that students worked on. It allows me to see the nodes of a living project's structure. The 2013 set of student edits, nearly 9 years later, has 9.79 million article views. For a look at the dashboard, see Figure 3.1.

Figure 3.1. Wiki Education Dashboard View

3	17	268	22	9.57K	72⊕	9.79M	2⊕
Articles Created	Articles Edited	Total Edits	Student Editors	Words Added	References Added	Article Views	Commons Uploads

Screenshot from Wiki Dashboard, fall 2013, accessed January 2023 (data reflects 2018 statistics). This figure demonstrates the typical dashboard statistics on student contributions available through the Wiki Education program.

Nine-point-seven-nine million article views. The number makes me pause.

Nine-point-seven-nine million people have viewed the pages where 22 Diablo Valley Community College students, in a night course on composition and literature, contributed to the history of the literature of the Harlem Renaissance (accessed 2022, December 24) from a semester-long study of the subject. If I close my eyes, I can hear and see those students, tucked under the fluorescent lights of a quiet library that held the door past 9 P.M. for as long as it could. They nervously open the back end of Wikipedia, learn how to code entries, and add content piece by piece, citation by citation, to the world's largest encyclopedia and one of most trafficked search engines globally (Purdy, 2020). Some students band together to start a page on Arthur P. Davis (2023), an important African American editor and scholar of the Harlem Renaissance. Another student adds content to Georgia Douglas Johnson (2023), a significant poet. Other students click through the pages and volumes of W. E. B. Du Bois's *The Crisis* (2023), to find what they might contribute, not quite sure where to start the process.

I remember students' worries: *Can I really do this? . . . Wait, how do I do this? . . . Won't someone just erase this research work? . . . I've never been to this side of Wikipedia before!* As much as Wikipedia was familiar, the other side of the button—the editing side—was unknown and unexplored.

One student in her late thirties, who was returning to school to pursue nursing, was a bright, interesting, serious student in the way our working students often are at the community college. She wanted to contribute to the Harlem Renaissance page but expressed that she was nervous because the page was heavily trafficked. I remember when she told me her goal, I, too, got a little nervous. There is a lot at stake on that page—a representation of a much larger and significant history that captures one of the most influential global movements in arts and literature. Could she contribute? Could she steward the importance of that page carefully?

Moreover, this particular student wanted to write about religion, a topic that can send red flags to Wikipedia editors because of the complexity of shaping religious materials and histories with neutrality. In the context of Harlem Renaissance literature, Christian tropes—the difficult role of faith, themes of exodus, exile, and resurrection—were important for a world undergoing a racial reawakening. The representation of Christianity during the Harlem Renaissance is multidimensional. For some writers, Christlike figures offered the possibility of rebirth. For other writers, Christianity in African American cultures reflected the history of slavery and forced removal from Africa. Countee Cullen's poem, "Heritage," (1925) asks the question, "What is Africa to me?" and recognizes that, as a son of slaves, the speaker's inherited distance from Africa and ancestral conversion to Christianity has come "high-priced." In our crowded room, with the hum of stationary computers, and the night bright outside, this 30-year-old returning nursing student mapped these layers of Christianity in the Harlem Renaissance into Wikipedia. She added the heading "Religion" and the subheadings "Discourse" and "Criticism." I was struck and inspired by this student's boldness and felt lucky to witness her strength. If the entry was erased, so be it. That erasure would tell us something about the way research operates in the 21st century in digital structures. I had to remember why we did this Wikipedia project in the first place—to see if we *could.*

And she did. Still to this day, the student's section, and her architectural understanding of the discourse on religion, remains. The section has also been added to, changed, edited, and revised. I can see that new edits have pointed to additional scenarios, added more layers of citations, but I also see the structure and traces of the student's entry, and I am reminded of the care with which she etched that section many years ago in those twilight nights in the community college library.

GOING PUBLIC

I hope you are still doing the Harlem Renaissance projects! I still brag to my friends that I wrote in Wikipedia—the one we did in class.... I didn't realize it back then, but having that experience really helped me stand out in university classes and getting opportunities.

—Bidisha Nag, former student (personal communication, April 7, 2021).

In retrospect, one of the profound impacts of students contributing content to Wikipedia was their participation in the tangible reading, sculpting, and reporting of research. Wikipedia is essentially a research archive, a compendium of citations, a summary of research work. The site asks editors (contributors) to write a skillful synopsis of that research, an important task for outlining and framing *what is known*. To put this into the public's hands was what made Wikipedia one of the most innovative projects of the digital age—completely transforming how we access information, how we create that information, and who gets to participate in that creation and transcription. That "who" element is the particular root of this transformation. It challenges the concept of who participates in the production of expertise. When I think of my students' work, I see them helping to shape important histories through their own editorial observations—selecting, deciphering, and interpreting the research that they believe is important.

I recall that in Spring 2018, my students were particularly fascinated by our reading of Nella Larsen's *Passing*—a brilliant Harlem Renaissance novel for teaching research, reflection, and the excitement of reading. Many students were drawn to the scholarly research around the work, which opened up themes that spoke to them—class, race, sexuality, fluid identity, friendship, and even jealousy. Several students chose to contribute summaries of this scholarship around these topics to the Wikipedia page on *Passing* (2023). In these contributions, students act as builders, moving into a more public dialogue of what they observe, what resonates, and what they see as valuable in these scholarly readings of this novel.

Sometimes the students' work is less present, small etches and remnants. Sometimes the work has disappeared, absorbed into a revision, or removed. As James Purdy (2009) writes, "Wikipedia (and wikis more generally) asks us to reexamine our expectations for the stability of research materials and who should participate in public knowledge making" (p. 352). The work in this realm is not fossilized, nor is participation reliant on a vetted system or hierarchy of knowledge certification or degree. Wikipedia, as a crowdsourced platform, offers participants an opportunity for citizen research.

CITIZEN RESEARCH

I am pulling the idea of the citizen researcher from the term "citizen science" which points to the role that local and community voices play in capturing and entering scientific data (Vohland et al., 2021). The concept also draws from the wide body of work on digital citizenship (Buchholz et al., 2020). One of the oldest, U.S.-based examples of citizen science is the Cooperative Weather Station, an intricate network of volunteer-based observations on weather and climate established in 1890 (COOP). The data depend on a network that is able to access a wide array of areas—urban and rural—that may otherwise be inaccessible for the collection of routine data over a significant period of time. In the digital age, citizen science emerges in crowd-sourced apps. When citizens submit photos and observations through their phones, they contribute to databases which other researchers can draw from and analyze. Though professional scientists help to confirm the data, the science depends on the local participant's contribution. In Wikipedia, contributors do not provide original research, but their discoveries and observations are important factors in the building and dissemination of knowledge. In students' hands, contributing to Wikipedia shifts knowledge authority from a hierarchical privilege of "discovery" and allows discovery to be local.

What is also clear is that "citizenship" and entry into "public" spheres are fraught with exclusionary systems. Access to Wikipedia's editorial tools entails a high level of digital literacy. When I began this project in 2013, students worked between Wiki markup (the Wikipedia-created language) and the newly built Visual Editor, an interface that allows editors to use familiar word processing features and tools to contribute. Wiki Edu, the educational arm of Wikipedia that connects higher education institutions with Wikipedia participation and content creation, had just formed and offered in-depth training and support. Still, the level of digital literacy required to enter this process is high.

There are other exclusions at play. Wikipedia has struggled and continues to struggle with diversifying editors and editorial contributions. There is a significant lack of representation from participants in the United States who identify within BIPOC, Latinx, AAPI, and other marginalized groups, and a significant overrepresentation of White contributors (Community and Newcomer Diversity, 2021). While approximately 85% of Wikipedia editors are men (Community and Newcomer Diversity, 2021), there are also modest gains in inclusion. Though still underrepresented, the proportion of women who are contributors increased from 11.5% of all editors in 2019 to 15% in 2020 (Community and Newcomer Diversity, 2021). Newcomers to Wikipedia, new editors from the past two years, tend to be more geographically diverse, though they do not necessarily continue to edit or contribute long term (Community Insights, 2021). Newcomers' feelings of empowerment increased overall and most significantly for new contributors in East Asia (Community Insights, 2021). See Figures 3.2 and 3.3.

Figure 3.2. Proportion of Women Contributors on Wikipedia

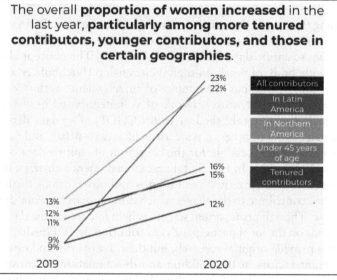

Graphic image by R. Maung (2021). Wikimedia Community Survey Insights 2021.

Figure 3.3. Geographic Representation Among Wiki Contributors

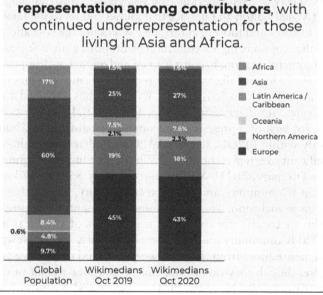

Table image by R. Maung (2021). Retrieved from Wikimedia Community Survey Insights 2021.

Calls to diversify and decolonize Wikipedia rightly focus on promoting contributions from Black, African American (Stewart et al., 2020), indigenous (Lugosi et al., 2022), and other marginalized community voices (Xing & Vetter, 2020). All note how adding to Wikipedia can be a form of social justice work (Carwil-Bjork, 2021). The community college system is a significant starting place for this work. Community college demographics reflect a very diverse set of students racially, ethnically, and socioeconomically (CCC Key Facts, 2023). They also reflect diversity of language, experience, age, and college status such as first-in-family to attend college. I remember a distinct moment in a Wikipedia presentation, around 2014, detailing the organization's work to connect to higher education, during which the speaker scrolled through a montage of elite colleges that had participated in editorial work—Harvard, UC Berkeley, NYU, Tufts, Georgetown. Almost no community colleges were listed at that time, and they still remain a small percentage of contributors. If the call from Wikipedia is to create an inclusive environment, promote "knowledge equity" (Collaboration, Diversity, and Inclusion, 2021, para 13), and bring along people who have been excluded by structures of power and privilege, who better to support the work of building inclusivity than members of the community college system? My students are Latinx, African, African American, Filipino, Tibetan, Middle Eastern, Chinese, Russian, and White. They are workers, returning students, grandmothers, mothers, fathers, high schoolers, students living with disabilities, and LGBTQIA+ identified. These are the voices that can build and shape the intricacies of dispossessed histories.

STUDENT AUTHORITY AND PARTICIPATORY LITERACIES

The real heart of this project is not Wikipedia; it is opening a space for students to experiment with their own authority in technological literacies, language, history, and culture. The project connects students through "networked technologies" (Leu & Kinzer, 2000) to what is known across the globe, the way a spider web builds its beautiful silk structure. If we blink, we miss all the intricacies, inconsistencies, and variances of how these webs are formed. But if we see the web structure in a moment where the sun and dew make it visible, then we witness an extraordinary and powerful view into how information is shared, exchanged, and structured online.

Within our community college classroom, the Wikipedia project subverts the idea of students waiting and writing outside the gates of academic research. In participating in open-source work, students have the opportunity to claim academic authority. They have the chance to help build how the world will read and see, in this case, the history of the Harlem Renaissance. I remember my fear of this visibility. Are my students prepared for this responsibility? Am I prepared to help them navigate that responsibility? Is the academic world ready for the students? In many ways, each answer is both *yes and no*. One action that helped me move forward, even when I was hesitant about what students would generate, was to acknowledge that research is living and imperfect. Moreover, if I acknowledge that classroom power should shift, then my focus is on helping students participate in the exchange and dialogue around production and delivery, and not on *determining who I think is ready* by reinforcing gatekeeping structures that have kept academic knowledge exclusive. As my students participate in the work of Wikipedia, they will run into, and create, loose ends, weak spots, failures of structure, errors, and issues. They will also fix many of these loose ends by adding in citations, fixing sentences, updating data and timelines, and reworking structures to make them clearer. See Figure 3.4.

Figure 3.4. Wikipedia Dashboard View of Georgia Douglas Johnson Page

Georgia Douglas Johnson, Spring 2017, course edits accessed January 2023. Note the call for "additional citations"—at times students addressed these calls as well as, at times, created them.

The project benefits from the process of review and revision, and, in this way, is a much more accurate reflection of actual work that takes place across global systems of digital exchange. Robert Cummings (2020) calls this exchange "public review" (p. 951), the way in which the open-sourced system of editors—plus a clear statement on the processes and procedures of contribution—invites fluid revision. Students see their work in conjunction with an ongoing stream of contribution that extends far beyond their initial edits. Wikipedia's editorial history creates a sophisticated record of research review in which the traces of interaction, change, and even erasures are present. See Figure 3.5.

Figure 3.5. Editorial History on Countee Cullen's Wikipedia Page

- (cur I prev) ○   01:26, 26 May 2017 Vargasv1920 (talk I contribs) . . (26,502 bytes) (+2,632) . . *(Add Literary Influe*

- (cur I prev) ○   01:22, 26 May 2017 Vargasv1920 (talk I contribs) . . (23,870 bytes) (+2,968) . . *(Add Major Works :* *Christ subsection)* (undo I thank) *(Tag: Visual edit)*

- (cur I prev) ○   01:16, 26 May 2017 Vargasv1920 (talk I contribs) . . (20,902 bytes) (+555) . . *(Add subheading "Ch plagiarism and add more information on Cullen's early life)* (undo I thank) *(Tag: Visual edit)*

- (cur I prev) ○   01:12, 26 May 2017 Vargasv1920 (talk I contribs) . . (20,347 bytes) (−11) . . *(Add more information*

- (cur I prev) ○   17:09, 25 May 2017 Jonadelsarol (talk I contribs) . . (20,358 bytes) (+17) . . *(corrected citations)* (u

- (cur I prev) ○   17:08, 25 May 2017 Jonadelsarol (talk I contribs) . . (20,341 bytes) (−496) . . (undo I thank) *(Tag: Vi*

- (cur I prev) ○   17:06, 25 May 2017 Jonadelsarol (talk I contribs) . . (20,837 bytes) (−214) . . (undo I thank) *(Tag: Vi*

- (cur I prev) ○   17:05, 25 May 2017 Jonadelsarol (talk I contribs) . . (21,051 bytes) (−207) . . *(→Relationships)* (un

- (cur I prev) ○   17:01, 25 May 2017 Jonadelsarol (talk I contribs) . . (21,258 bytes) (+257) . . *(→Sexuality)* (undo I t

- (cur I prev) ○   16:49, 25 May 2017 Jonadelsarol (talk I contribs) . . (21,001 bytes) (+2,415) . . *(Added sexuality ar.*

- (cur I prev) ○   16:54, 21 May 2017 173.61.129.206 (talk) . . (18,586 bytes) (+1) . . *(→Color)* (undo)

- (cur I prev) ○   19:47, 17 May 2017 Qchapple (talk I contribs) m . . (18,585 bytes) (+951) . . *(Added information.)* (

- (cur I prev) ○   19:10, 17 May 2017 Qchapple (talk I contribs) m . . (17,634 bytes) (+15) . . *(Re-organizing the sub* Visual edit)

- (cur I prev) ○   17:44, 16 May 2017 Qchapple (talk I contribs) m . . (17,619 bytes) (+25) . . *(reorganization)* (undo I

- (cur I prev) ○   17:30, 16 May 2017 Qchapple (talk I contribs) m . . (17,594 bytes) (−197) . . *(Edited the citations a.*

Countee Cullen editorial history snapshot of 2017, accessed January 2023, showing that student editors at the community college across different classrooms as well as external Wikipedia editors intersect and collaborate (Countee Cullen: Revision History, 2023).

One of the pushbacks for the use of the encyclopedia is the question of "credibility." Because Wikipedia decentralizes authorship, there is not a single point person or group that is responsible for the information. Credibility depends on the ongoing collaborative practices of its editors and the maintenance of digital literacies to keep it accessible. In the anxiety to maintain credibility, editors consistently collaborate, maintain, monitor, and revise. To assist, Wikipedia provides clear principles of editorial practices and participation (Wikipedia Five Pillars & Wikipedia Policies and Guidelines). Moreover, Wiki.edu has created a series of well-designed training modules that onboard students to the platform and to editing practices. Students learn how these pages operate, how the community operates, and what it means to participate. Equally important, however, is the principle, "ignore all rules," which states: "If a rule prevents you from improving or maintaining Wikipedia, **ignore it**" (Ignore All Rules, 2023). This keeps the site open, flexible, and therefore, living.

In the site's fluidity, my students often struggled with the process of moving through public participatory research. In end-of-project reflective essays, students documented their experiences with the project. They often noted the following challenges and opportunities:

Challenges:

1. *Selecting where and what to contribute; selecting topics or articles where students could make the most impact*
2. *Adding to preexisting work, determining what to add or fix*
3. *Evaluating the credibility of research materials summarized and cited on the platform*
4. *Writing objectively and adhering to the concept of neutrality when reporting on researched information*
5. *Navigating image copyright and understanding the boundaries of what counts as "open-access"*
6. *Feeling confident (or not feeling confident) to participate in an open, public source*

Opportunities:

1. *A deeper sense of the history and culture of the Harlem Renaissance*
2. *A deeper ability to read Wikipedia in terms of structure, content, and form*
3. *A deeper understanding of how citations operate*
4. *An urgency to correct the "flaws" and citation gaps they saw on Wikipedia*
5. *A stronger appreciation for how information is generated online*
6. *A feeling of pride or admiration for their contributions*

My students also often commented on their awareness that their contributions would be read and seen by potentially millions of people. They expressed a sense of "responsibility" as well as anxiety—*would they be erased?* Or, perhaps even more so, *would they be read?* They were proud of their contributions and wanted them to be read. In fact, they reported that the act of someone reading their work was equally frightening and exhilarating. One way I like to think of the students' contributions is to imagine them as a language and research lab with an experiment in play where the students might experience successful or failed results. Regardless of initial hypothesis, the information produced within the lab tells us something about research and researchers in real time. The project gave students a glimpse of how language could have power and how they could contribute to something larger than themselves and the classroom. The project illuminates their voice on a larger stage.

I want to reiterate. It is so important that community college students' voices are on that larger stage.

PARTICIPATORY RESEARCH AS A LIVING STRUCTURE

As I scroll back through the Wikipedia dashboards of my various classes, I am reminded that the contributions the students made continue to live on through the participatory structure of digital research in the 21st century. Rather than mimicking the closed boundary of the traditional classroom research paper, the students' work continues to generate impact and underscores the notion that digital literacies include knowledge of technologies that are participatory, collaborative, networked, and driven by digital citizenship (Buchholz et al., 2020; Leu & Kinzer, 2000; Milenkova & Lendzhova, 2021; Yancey, 2009). I also acknowledge that 21st century digital literacies can be problematic, exclusive, and can reinforce systemic systems of race, class, gender, and sexuality. Witnessing community college students contribute to the public history of the Harlem Renaissance within Wikipedia is an invitation to strengthen digital literacies and an antidote to closed learning systems.

When I read the Wikipedia page on Georgia Douglas Johnson (2023)—a wonderful but often forgotten poet of the Harlem Renaissance—I see traces of my students' research continuing to live on: their interest in her marriage and the tie between creative work and domestic work; her central place in the creation of the S Street Salon; her participation in antilynching activism. In seeing what they saw and how they helped build her page—and in doing so, her history—I see their voices, their craft, their connection to others, their web, that is so intrinsic to diversifying the kinds of histories we encourage and the kinds of research practices we build as writing educators.

CONCLUSION

I remember my trepidation when I first introduced Wikipedia—as a writing project—into my English composition courses. It felt like I was breaking the academic code that says, "Don't use Wikipedia for research." I also knew that I wanted to invite my students to think about, as well as participate in, new digital literacies beyond a traditional academic or research essay. I wanted them to have a voice in these discussions more than I wanted to uphold an academic code. After all, breaking rules is a kind of breakthrough.

I hope this essay invites discussion, conversation, and even community-building around what types of projects we can assign that might ask students to explore digital realms of information access, exchange, and participation. In my own example, empowering community college students to add to the history of the Harlem Renaissance helped contribute to a wider mosaic of this period of literature, art, and music that represents the vast beauty, strength, struggles, and power of that time.

A project like this is not confined to the Harlem Renaissance. Imagine this assignment's impact on other marginalized histories. Even focusing on a school's local community history can allow students to connect and deepen their relationships to each other as well as to the surrounding area. Partnerships with local librarians, archives, and other community resource groups could help build histories that might otherwise remain silent, forgotten, or underrepresented.

I also want to note that a project like this is not limited to Wikipedia. I hope this essay encourages many kinds of conversation about where digital literacy and participatory culture intersect inside the classroom. There are many types of projects that ask students to contribute to digital networks of information building and exchange. For example, there are other open-source platforms such as Open Street Maps, which, like Wikipedia, invite its users to tag information to maps in order to enrich geographical representation. Open archival transcription projects, such as those offered by the Library of Congress, invite students, or public volunteers, to contribute to historical access by transcribing archival documents.

Why Wikipedia? In projects like this, it is inevitable that students (and instructors) will make mistakes. Projects may snag and technology may glitch or fail. Digital platforms may have their own limitations. That said, giving students the tools and practice to contribute to an open-source digital platform can give them the confidence and authority to navigate and discuss those challenges with you and with each other, affirming that their written work and research matters in tangible and profound ways.

RECOMMENDED READING

Carwil-Bjork, J. (2021). New maps for an inclusive Wikipedia: Decolonial scholarship and strategies to counter systemic bias. *New Review of Hypermedia and Multimedia*, 27(3), 207–228.

> Carwil-Bjork's conference talk, which later became this (2021) article, explains how Wikipedia can help create new "maps" of knowledge by shifting who participates and contributes to knowledge geographies.

Cook, J. M. (2021, April 30). Students bring indigenous perspectives to Wikipedia. *University of Alberta's Folio.* https://www.ualberta.ca/folio/2021/04/students-bring -indigenous-perspectives-to-wikipedia.html.

Cook's (2021) article highlights Nykkie Lugosi-Schimpf's use of Wikipedia in the classroom to introduce the histories, voices, theories, and practices of Indigenous populations and communities.

Montez, N. (2017). Decolonizing Wikipedia through advocacy and activism: The Latina/o Theatre Wikiturgy Project. *Theatre Topics, 27*(1), E-1. https://doi .org/10.1353/tt.2017.0012

Montez' (2017) article showcases the work he and his students undertook to build more representation of Latinx theater on Wikipedia and the tensions the project revealed about Wikipedia's editorial limitations.

About Chapter 4

Eleventh grade social studies teacher **Stan Pesick** finds himself mired in student research papers that are dry, rote, and painful to read. After several attempts to come up with alternatives, he breaks through the bottleneck of tradition by putting his students in the role of investigators of a moment in time that intrigues them—a moment when they might say "I wish I'd been there."

What characterizes Pesick's breakthrough is the authority he gives students to come to history—not as a done deal—but as something to question, to explore, to shake free of accepted interpretations that might not stand up in the light of what we know now. He finds a legitimacy for his students' research and writing—something that promises a meaningful experience beyond a school assignment—and a way for students to make judgments about historical significance and consequences.

CHAPTER 4

Looking Backward

How the "Fly on the Wall" Changed My History Instruction

Stan Pesick

The conversation often goes like this: I'm at some kind of social gathering and start talking to someone I've just met. "What do you do?" "I teach history in high school." "Oh, I hated history." I never know quite how to respond, but I know that I didn't want my students to repeat that same refrain. And I also know that investigating the reasons behind the "I hated history" comment was the focus of a number of studies and commentaries. Here's a sampling of some of the findings: According to James Loewen (1995)

> Students consider history 'the most irrelevant' of twenty-one school subjects commonly taught in high school. 'Borr-r-ring' is the adjective they apply to it. When students can, they avoid it, even though most students get higher grades in history than in math, science, or English. Even when they are forced to take classes in history, they repress what they learn, so every year or two another study decries what our seventeen-year-olds don't know. (p.12)

Another study concludes, that as far as most students are concerned, the required social studies knowledge consists of nothing more than "assertions that are either true or false, correct or incorrect, right or wrong" (Kornfeld & Goodman, 1998, p. x). And, as of this writing, when history teachers in a number of states and districts around the nation are being denied the opportunity to raise certain historical questions connected to race, religion, nationality, gender, and sexuality, along with questions of freedom and democracy (Schwartz, 2022), we may sadly see another reason for the "I hated history class" comment.

Every history teacher—past and present—faces the challenge of breaking through the "I hate history" barrier. Whatever our larger goals—and I certainly had mine—we have to conquer the myth that history is just names and facts. In my case, I hoped my students would leave my class with a sense that their time there was well spent. That our work with history was both exciting and challenging. That what they learned was important to both them and their classmates. How to do this? My breakthrough came slowly, painfully, and sometimes accidentally.

FROM UNINSPIRED HISTORY PAPERS TO A BREAKTHROUGH

In 1976 I was fresh out of teacher training when I started teaching at one of the large comprehensive high schools in Oakland, California. The student population of my school represented the population of the neighborhood in which it was situated. There was an African American majority, a large number of Mexican Americans, a handful of Whites, and the beginnings of a Southeast Asian immigrant population.

During those years I taught 11th-grade U.S. history. In our department we used a portion of this course to teach students how to write a research paper. I thought about how I learned to do research when I was in high school. My teachers passed out a series of topics, gave us a few guidelines in regard to length and format, and said come back in a month with a paper. Like the process I remembered, I listed about forty possible topics from U.S. history, such as "The Reasons for the Civil War," "Life During the Depression," "The Impact of the Automobile," and so on. Though the topics could be interesting, this method was not successful with my students. What I got back from the students was, at best, the encyclopedia—our main resource at the time—rearranged and paraphrased or, at worst, the encyclopedia and other books copied word for word. Needless to say, many of the papers I received were not a great read, lacking the detail, the sense of story, and the committed voice of the historian. The students' writing was not at all like the historical writing I enjoyed reading and hoped my students would learn to appreciate and create. This should not have been surprising. At this point in their academic careers, the textbook, along with the encyclopedia, seemed to be the only models of historical writing most students could draw upon. No wonder their writing suffered.

I have no doubt that most students worked hard on these papers. In this pre-Internet time, going to the library, checking out books and journals, and paraphrasing or copying took time and effort. But in the end, no matter how hard they worked, most didn't care about the words they were writing. Indeed, some students even asked, as they prepared to write, "Do you want this in my words?" It was a very frustrating situation for both teacher and students.

It was clear that the process I learned in high school was not going to get the results I wanted. It was also clear that a good number of students, perhaps most, lacked many of the research skills necessary to write an insightful and engaging paper. Doing the research, selecting the information, developing a position or argument, and then arranging it in an interesting and thoughtful way was a daunting challenge. In effect, my assignment had sent the students on a not-so-scenic journey without the road signs or maps needed to help them arrive at the destination I had in mind. So moving beyond my own personal experience, I went out and found some "how to" manuals. One I found was *10 Steps in Writing the Research Paper* (Markham & Waddell, 1971). It provided some generally sound advice: how to select a topic, how to formulate a thesis statement, how to take notes from relevant sources, and how to write the first draft. I integrated this advice into my research paper instruction, looking forward to improvement. But once again that next set of papers rarely included passages where a historian's voice was heard amid the din of names, dates, places, and events. And maybe most important, the students didn't see the writing of history as a place for curiosity and imagination, or as a place to get in their "two cents."

Still trying to find ways to help students improve their writing of history, I attended the Bay Area Writing Project Summer Institute at the University of California, Berkeley in 1979. During that summer I heard practical suggestions on how to help students develop questions to focus their research, and how to help students go through the process of writing, revising, and editing. Optimistically, I put a number of these suggestions to use by putting together a new and improved "research paper packet" that outlined a detailed step-by-step process. Once again, the papers, for the most part, still lacked the kind of historical writing and thinking I wanted to read. In response, I decided, quite wrongly as it turned out, to double down on the process of doing the paper.

This time everyone would write on a topic I selected, and in preparation, read the same articles and books. We worked as a class to take notes from these common readings and put together a common outline. Finally, after all this work was done, each student wrote his or her own paper. Unfortunately, but in hindsight quite predictably, this process resulted in sixty versions of the same paper that all said the same thing. Once again, individual engagement and the historian's voice was missing. It was kind of like listening to a chorus in which everyone was singing off-key simultaneously. And, to top it off, I needed to read and comment on each of them.

BREAKTHROUGH #1—"I WISH I'D BEEN THERE"

Sometime after "the class writes the same paper" approach, I came across an article in *American Heritage* magazine. The magazine asked a number of working historians and writers to write about one event in American history they would like to have witnessed as a "fly on a wall" (1984). Below are two examples from that issue.

Witchcraft

Maybe it's my Quaker ancestry (on the paternal side) that has me choosing personally to witness a small jewel of a thing which happened in nascent Pennsylvania on February 27, 1684. Back then, it seems, Quakers were not altogether immune to the witch-mindedness of their day; and here was an elderly woman, doubtless psychotic, on trial for witchcraft. William Penn, creator of the colony and temporarily a resident there, lent his proprietary presence and took part in examining the accused.

"Art thou a witch?" he asked her. "Hast thou ever ridden through the air on a broomstick?" The poor old thing insisted that indeed she had. Penn told her in effect that he knew of no law against it and recommended that the jury dismiss her. So they found her guilty not of witchcraft but merely of having the "common fame of being a witch" and set her free.

To have been there would have shown what must have been the most benevolent poker face ever seen. Further, this was probably the most civilized thing to have occurred on the North American continent since Columbus's landing—a spontaneous leap ahead of the terms of the time. And for relish, I don't doubt the old lady hobbled away pretty huffy about not having been taken seriously. (Furnas, 1984, p. 27)

Emancipation

The incident that I would have witnessed is that described in Thomas Wentworth Higginson's *Army Life in a Black Regiment*. He writes of a ceremony in South Carolina on January 1, 1863, celebrating the coming into effect of the Emancipation Proclamation. The ceremony was conventional and simple until Higginson got up to speak and waved the American flag before the audience of black soldiers, white civilians and officers, and a large number of slaves, who at the moment were legally receiving their freedom for the first time. As the flag was being waved, Higginson tells us, "there arose . . . a strong male voice (but rather cracked and elderly), into which two women's voices instantly blended, singing, as if by an impulse that could no more be repressed than the morning note of the song sparrow-'My Country, 'tis of thee, Sweet Land of Liberty, of thee I sing!'"

The ceremony ended as the former slaves sang on, irrepressibly, through verse and verse. Higginson motioned the few whites who began to join in to be silent. The moment, as he said, was electric. "Nothing could be more wonderfully unconscious; art could not have dreamt of a tribute to the day of jubilee that should be so affecting; history will not believe it . . ." This incident epitomizes the most profound moment in America's social history: that point when millions ceased to be slaves in the home of the free and set in motion the historic challenge that white America make real its own vision. (Degler, 1984, p.32)

In each of these, the historian's voice, built on vivid description, source analysis, and interpretation, is loud and clear. With these examples in mind, I began to rethink how I approached the research project. I asked myself what would happen if I gave more choice in what to investigate? Would that create more engagement, both personal and academic, with the writing and the content?

With these questions in mind, I began the new research paper assignment with the question "What event or scene in 20th century American history would you like to have witnessed and why?"

Initially, the new assignment resulted in some interesting papers that started to take on an historian's voice, but there were still problems to work out. One challenge was that many students didn't know a great deal about specific events in the 20th century and they had a hard time getting specific and detailed in their writing. For example, students wanted to be at D-Day, or in Montgomery during the bus boycott, or in Vietnam. These were great topics, but much too big. Like the preceding examples, I wanted students to delve into a very specific historical moment.

I don't remember exactly how I came to this idea, but I began to tackle this problem by beginning the assignment with a photograph or illustration. This meant the students' first steps would be to identify a photo or illustration of a specific historic event, describe the event in detail, and then develop an inquiry question about this particular historical moment. See Figure 4.1 for the assignment.

Figure 4.1. The Assignment

"I WISH I'D BEEN THERE"
WHAT IS THE ONE SCENE OR EVENT IN 20th CENTURY AMERICAN HISTORY YOU WOULD LIKE TO HAVE WITNESSED—AND WHY?

Begin your work by selecting a photograph or a painting of a particular event and developing an historical inquiry question about this event.

Your final paper should seek to answer your historical question by:

- Describing the event
- Explaining the historical context in which it took place (narration)
- Analyzing its significance to the historical period and U.S. history
- Explaining why you want to have witnessed this event. Why does it so intrigue you?

Attached are a few examples of how some professional historians answered this question. Read their responses over to get some ideas on how you might approach this assignment. These examples are taken from the article, "I Wish I'd Been There," which appeared in *American Heritage* magazine December, 1984.

Starting with a photograph turned out to be a big help to students who now had something very concrete to investigate. Rather than be at D-Day, students could choose to be on the beach at Normandy; rather than being in Montgomery during the bus boycott, students could choose to be on the bus with Rosa Parks. A photo was a great aid in narrowing the topic. As students chose their photographs, they instantly engaged with the subject. Or, as Alfred North Whitehead wrote, this engagement led to a kind of "romance" with the subject which he argued was a first step towards precision (Whitehead, 1929). I learned my students had a much better chance of success if they investigated an event they really wanted to learn about and understand.

Figures 4.2 and 4.3 provide two examples of how my students, having selected a photo, explored their questions about the event portrayed and its significance. In the first example, my student "Stephanie" invokes democratic ideals from her engagement with the photo she chose. In the second, "Shannon" imagines taking part in a historic event, the March on Washington.

Stephanie used the photo in Figure 4.2 of Yuki Okinaga Hayakawa waiting for the train taking her and her mother from Los Angeles to Manzanar incarceration camp, as a starting place for her inquiry. She wanted to know how Japanese Americans endured the hardships of being taken from their homes and having their freedom taken away. She wrote about how she, like many Japanese Americans, was raised on democratic beliefs and ideals, and could only imagine their anger over losing their

Figure 4.2. A Young Evacuee Waits with the Family Baggage before Leaving for an Assembly Center (Albers, 1942)

Figure 4.3. March on Washington (Trikoso, 1963)

rights. In addition, Stephanie also sought answers to how this cruel act could happen. Her inquiry led her to the report from the Commission on Wartime Relocation and Internment of Civilians (CWRIC) that concluded Executive Order 9066 was not justified by military necessity but rather was the result of "race prejudice, war hysteria, and a failure of political leadership." Stephanie ended her discussion by arguing that unless we uphold Constitutional protections for all, we are in danger of allowing such a terrible mistake to happen again.

The photo in Figure 4.3, taken at the August 1963 March on Washington, shows a group of marchers and the signs they held. Shannon used the photo to imagine what she would have experienced had she been there. She wrote about how wonderful it would be to feel the passion and exhilaration she saw on the faces of the marchers and commented on how the messages on their signs reflected who was there and why. Through this analysis she contextualized this moment within a history of racism she wanted to see ended. She noted all the different kinds of people in the photo, and tried to articulate what united them at this historic event. She interspersed her narrative with passages from Dr. King's speech:

> *I have a dream that one day this nation will rise up and live out the true meaning of its creed: "We hold these truths to be self-evident, that all men are created equal."*
>
> *. . . [W]hen we allow freedom ring, when we let it ring from every village and every hamlet, from every state and every city, we will be able to speed up that*

day when all of God's children, black men and white men, Jews and Gentiles, Protestants and Catholics, will be able to join hands and sing. . . . (King, 1963, reprinted by KQED, 2023, para 21).

The last lines of her paper are taken from the last lines of King's speech.

Free at last! Free at last!

Thank God Almighty, we are free at last! (King, 1963, reprinted by KQED, 2023, para 30).

The beauty of photos, as the previous accounts illustrate, is their power to pinpoint a significant moment in time.

EVALUATING HISTORICAL SIGNIFICANCE

The core of the assignment is a response to an inquiry question that asks for an evaluation, a judgment of historical significance. The following questions highlight elements for identifying events of historical significance (adapted from Lévesque, 2008).

- Was the event important to people who lived then? Why? In what ways?
- How deeply were people affected by the event? Was it profound and deeply affecting? How did it impact hopes, fears, and other concerns?
- Was the impact of the event long-lasting or only short-lived?
- Is the event relevant to our understanding of the past and/or present?

Judgments of historical significance are made by people living in the present looking back at the past. As Peter Seixas argues, "standards of significance apparently inhere not only in the past itself, but in the interpretative frames and values of those who study it—ourselves" (Lévesque, 2008, p. 44). I saw this idea at work in both the writing of the professional historians and the students.

BREAKTHROUGH #2—THE CORE ASSIGNMENT

To prepare students for Fly on the Wall, I revised the role the textbook—which was the major resource at the time—played in my classroom. I wanted the students to use their reading as a point of departure for historical inquiry, to get away from the idea that a single source provided was the final word about an historical event or person. I also wanted them to have a lot of practice, so I started the core assignment at the beginning of the school year and repeated it eight or nine times during the year. See the core assignment in Figure 4.4.

Figure 4.4. Core Assignment—Preparing for the "Fly on the Wall"

Part I—Select a total of **five** important individuals, groups, or events that you would regard as **historically significant**. Use either of the following criteria to justify each of your selections.

> 1) Significant events and people are those which have the greatest impact, either positive or negative, on the lives of individuals and groups in a particular time period.
> 2) Significant events and people are those which relate in some way to us, in the present, who are doing the historical thinking.

Part II—React to the reading by recording:

- Questions you have about the material covered in the reading.
- Reactions you have to the particular events and people (select at least one event and one person.)
- Two particular phrases or sentences which you want to remember— write down the phrase and explain why you selected it. Why is the phrase significant?
- Anything else which comes to mind as you read.

Part III—Select the photo or illustration in these pages that most interests you and write a paragraph that:

- Describes what you see in the illustration **(to describe means to make a person or event come to life through the use of vivid details).**
- Explains why the picture is in the chapter. How is it connected to this specific time period or event?
- Discusses why the picture interests you.

PREPARING FOR HISTORICAL INQUIRY

Below are some examples of questions from the core assignment that 11th-grade students asked in response to a chapter that focused on westward expansion. They illustrate how even a textbook might be used to generate questions worth investigating if students are reading closely and thinking deeply about the history they encounter.

- *Why couldn't Supreme Court Justice John Marshall enforce his ruling?*
- *Why did the Cherokees abandon their ideas and change their lifestyle?*
- *Why were the settlers so inclined to leave where they were from? Did something happen to them? Why did they want to leave?*

- *The United States didn't want their land (or rights) taken by the British. They knew what it was like to be threatened. Why would they threaten someone else?*
- *If the U.S. government took the time to protect the Native Americans in the Northwest Ordinance (1787) why didn't they follow through with it?*

These questions weren't the only ones students asked; there were many that asked for clarification of content and vocabulary. What sets these questions apart is that they can only be answered with further study and discussion. These questions suggest an engagement in the material that would either be invisible or absent if the students were simply asked to answer the textbook questions that often appear at the end of a chapter or text section.

STUDENTS PRACTICE WORKING WITH AN IMAGE

Part III of the assignment asks students to select and comment on an image or photo that is included in the text section they are reading. Figure 4.5 shows a 1942 painting depicting the 1838 Cherokee Trail of Tears (Lindneux, 1942).

Figure 4.5. Trail of Tears (Lindneux, 1942)

Here is how one student, "May," explored the connection between the words she was reading and the image.

After reading the section, "The Cherokee Solution," I was not only out-raged, but also disgusted by the unthoughtful ways Southern whites treated the Cherokee because they were hungry to obtain Cherokee land. It was bad enough that settlers took away land that didn't belong to them, but they went a little further by pushing off the Cherokee into the desert. The settlers them-selves came to the colonies in search of a new life and experience the feelings of striking it rich by owning farms and so on . . . they settled in a new land because they were deprived of what they wanted and in doing so, the Native Americans were deprived of what they have. . . . If settlers had thought of that, maybe they would have taken smaller and easier steps in their westward expansion.

The situation faced by the Cherokee caught my attention and I would like to do further study of the tribe because I am very eager to learn what became of them after their removal. Being an immigrant from Vietnam, I experienced the hardship of my trail of tears when my family and I and thousands of my people left our country because of communism. We found a better life in the United States after we left our mother land. But what about the Cherokee, did they find a better life after they left theirs? And what happened to them today? This is what I would like to learn.

In this example, May develops an argument about the historical sig-nificance of the Cherokee removal, and raises additional questions for in-vestigation. She understands the profound impact this event had on the Cherokee, and wonders how the settlers, given their own experiences, could do this to another group of people. Significantly, she connects this event to the experiences of her own family. In doing so, she illustrates a desire to move beyond her own cultural borders and seek some common ground with another group of people. Through their study of history, the students were beginning to learn, as May's writing on the Cherokee Trail of Tears il-lustrates, how to cross the cultural boundaries set up by time and place, and in the process, develop historical understandings.

FINAL TAKE

So what is my final take on the Fly on the Wall assignment and the teach-ing that led up to it? Did it create more engagement and more meaningful research and writing?

My answer is a tentative "yes," but with two qualifications. First, while engagement became more apparent as revealed by both the types of ques-tions the students were asking and the comments they made, there was still a lot of work to do in terms of helping students develop the reading, writing, and thinking skills necessary to turn that engagement into thoughtful and insightful historical reading, writing, and thinking. That work fell on both the students and on me. The students worked on the "core activity" maybe eight or nine times during the year. And each time the assignments were turned in I followed up by selecting questions, comments, and interpretations from individual student papers to create a compilation of student writing that the whole class would read and discuss. These compilations were chosen with a goal of providing students examples that illustrated the thoughtful historical reading, writing, and thinking I was after. Through this process, I wanted students, using their own writing as a starting place, to learn how to read a historical text, how to formulate a historical inquiry question, how to work with historical evidence, and how to best articulate a historical understanding or argument. In addition, this process also meant students had frequent encounters with the multiple perspectives and questions articulated by their classmates. This was a significant consequence of my instructional breakthrough. As James Banks wrote, "The challenge that teachers face is how to make effective instructional use of the personal and cultural knowledge of students while at the same time helping them to reach beyond their own cultural boundaries" (1993, p. 8).

A second qualification connects to the role I played in all this work. If one of my goals was to have students be "in conversation" with the historical texts they were reading, it was important to take their questions and comments seriously and make this writing a focus of classroom discussion. Indeed, if students don't get to discuss the questions and ideas they are encouraged to articulate, they will probably stop asking and commenting.

CONCLUSION

This narrative of how I got to my breakthrough is, in reality, just the starting point for what I consider my most productive years of teaching. The work I'm describing here was neither teacher nor student centered. It was inquiry centered and that focus is the heart of teaching and learning history.

Although much has changed in how teachers organize, access, and present the content of their history courses since I taught these lessons almost 30 years ago, many of the challenges I cited are still with us. Indeed, how to engage students in historical inquiry, and then build on that engagement to advance students' ability to read, write, and think historically is still a core goal of history instruction. But, as mentioned at the start of this piece, for many teachers that goal can be undermined if they teach in school districts or states that seek to restrict the study of certain historical questions connected to race, religion, nationality, gender, and sexuality, along with questions of freedom and democracy (Schwartz, 2022). In grappling with these complex instructional challenges, I hope my colleagues see the importance of providing students the space to develop their own historical questions. Helping students develop the skills to craft, research, and then address those questions might make a difference in how students engage with the study of history, and how we as a nation collectively begin to understand, and not hide, the most challenging and troubling moments of our past.

RECOMMENDED READING

Kars, M. (1997). History in a grain of sand: Teaching the historian's craft. *The Journal of American History, 83*(4), 1340. https://doi.org/10.2307/2952905

> Marjoline Kars, a historian at the University of Maryland, writes, "Gradually students learn that any historical grain, even one in their own history, reflects the larger context in which it took place and can be made to speak to important questions in the past and the present." Kars' piece offers a narrative of how one teacher put this idea into practice.

Levine, L. W. (1989). The historian and the icon: Photography and the history of the American people in the 1930s and 1940s, *Documenting America, 1935–1943*. University of California Press. https://nationalhumanitiescenter.org/ows/seminars/tcentury/fsaphotos/levine.pdf

> Understanding a photograph not only depends on what the viewer sees, it depends on what the viewer sees in combination with trying to understand what the photographer wanted to communicate, and what the subject hoped would be revealed. In his essay, Levine explores this crucial insight for both teachers and students as they seek to understand the people who populate the history they investigate.

Miles, T. (2021). *All that she carried: The journey of Ashley's sack, a Black family keepsake*. Random House.

> In 1850s South Carolina, an enslaved woman named Rose faced a crisis, the imminent sale of her daughter Ashley. Thinking quickly, she packed a cotton bag with a few precious items as a token of love, and to try to ensure that Ashley survived. This bag was passed down from generation to generation.

Wilkerson, I. (2016). The long-lasting legacy of the great migration. *Smithsonian Magazine*. https://www.smithsonianmag.com/history/long-lasting-legacy-great-migration-180960118/

> A fine example of historical writing that integrates personal narratives, photographic images, and historical data. Wilkerson argues that the "Great Migration" of African Americans from the South to the North not only profoundly impacted the lives of those who made that journey and their descendants but also scattered seeds of hope that grew into the continued struggle for racial equality.

About Chapter 5

For **Kristin Land,** the pandemic brings with it the urgent need to make learning more joyful for her community college students, especially when contact is limited to Zoom. "I set out to center joy because I couldn't imagine how else I would entice my students—let alone myself—to show up each week if I didn't."

Land's breakthrough—reimagining her class in order to make a consistent space for joy and play—brings with it inevitable doubts. Is she doing justice to institutional expectations? A 2021 study about play in higher education provides one answer. While "playful pedagogy remains an uncommon approach" (Forbes, 2021, p. 57), one that is devalued and underused, when college students have the opportunity to experience play in the learning process, they are highly motivated and engaged, with no sacrifice of rigor. Land makes her own compelling case, with multiple classroom examples, for a practice she rightly calls "radical" and "transformative."

CHAPTER 5

Teach What You Love

How Carving Out Space for Joy Transforms a Composition Class

Kristin Land

During the early months of the pandemic, I made a vow to teach what I love and to have fun on Zoom.

I vowed to center fun—joy, really—in my Critical Thinking Through Literature community college course because I had been moved by Alice Walker's advice. "Hard times require furious dancing," she explains in the preface to her poetry collection with the same title. "Though we have all encountered our share of grief and troubles, we can still hold the line of beauty, form and beat—no small accomplishment in a world as challenging as this one" (2010, p. xv). Walker calls out a survival strategy used by marginalized communities for centuries: uplifting beauty and humanity ignites joy.

It is worth noting that joy is not synonymous with happiness. Psychologists describe joy as a deep state of well-being that arises from a clarity of purpose, from a sense of being in tune with something larger than ourselves. In *Burnout: The Secret to Unlocking the Stress Cycle*, Emily and Amelia Nagoski take that definition one step further, arguing that the very act of reminding others and ourselves that we are enough, just as we are, is the "springboard from which we launch into a joyful life" (Nagoski & Nagoski, 2020, p. 214). They insist, "Your joy matters. Please tell everyone you know" (p. 214).

That is what I set out to do: to greet my students, just as they are. I set out to show my mostly first-generation college students that there is joy in discovering our own interpretations of literature, that these discoveries have potential to connect us to our "something larger." I hoped to emphasize the beauty in discovering a new perspective, in conquering a challenge, in fine-tuning a skill, in seeing our family assets and ancestral wisdom elevated. But mostly, if I am honest, I set out to center joy because I couldn't imagine how else I would entice my students—let alone myself—to show up each week if I didn't.

I also wanted to entice students to stick out what would doubtless feel like a slog of a semester. Even in the best of times, there is no guarantee that my community college students will return to the next class. Students disappear midsemester. They are pulled away for a variety of reasons: a health challenge, a promotion at work, a new child, a desire to work in a more hands-on field, a responsibility to earn money for their household. I start every 18-week semester thinking of ways to dissuade students from dropping out, even when I am not teaching via a virtual platform. But, during the pandemic, the urgency to build a class full of sticky experiences, meaning activities that glue students to one another and to meaningful ideas, rose to a new height as community losses drove home for me what so many survivors of oppression understand intuitively: Joy is a resilience strategy.

CARVING SPACE FOR JOY

On a literal level, my vow to teach what I love and uplift joy meant I had to change aspects of my curriculum. I swapped out a play about Haitian children and replaced it with Luis Valdez's satirical, one-act plays: *Los Vendidos* and *The Militants* (1990). I replaced Jesmyn Ward's masterful but intense novel, *Sing, Unburied, Sing* (2018), with Weike Wang's cheeky novel, *Chemistry* (2017), a coming-of-age-story that opens with a rebuffed marriage proposal. I paired *Chemistry* with several short stories about relationships, including "Never Marry a Mexican" by Sandra Cisneros, "How to Date a Brown Girl" by Junot Diaz, and "Birthday" by David Wong Louie.

To deepen our analytical conversations about the literature, I integrated several chapters from bell hooks's essay collection *All about Love*. I was eager to hear how students felt about hooks's bold argument: "To truly love, we must learn to mix various ingredients—care, affection, recognition, respect, commitment, and trust, as well as honest and open communication" (hooks, 2001, pp. 5–6). My hope was that students would wrestle with and construct precise notions of what loving relationships might truly look like, a concept I believe is deeply useful for all adults, especially as we seek to confirm that our joy matters.

By setting out to teach both *what* I love and *about* love, I aimed to recreate a virtual environment with echoes of what I had experienced with my elementary school teacher, "Ms. Jarvis," back in 1985.

Schooling took a joyful turn for me when I entered Ms. Jarvis's 4th-grade classroom. Ms. Jarvis—whose guitar greeted us in the morning, whose walls lulled us with Dali's watches, whose lessons invited us to invent stories based on the witch my classmate drew—knew how to inspire. She gave us time to put our heads down on our desks and daydream until our pencils flurried across the page, depositing little haikus or illustrated comic strips. In her class, learning was a joyful process, a powerful blend of inquiry, creativity, and challenge individualized for each young mind's development. We took home jars of caterpillars that would become monarch butterflies, we bound books of our own words and drawings, we allowed art to spark our imaginations about life during the bubonic plague of the early Renaissance. Along with serious subjects, she melded joy.

Even though culturally her class was rooted in Eurocentric traditions, she seemed to hold onto the ancient beliefs that every individual's story matters, that every student's creative impulse deserves watering.

As 4th graders, we didn't produce Shakespeare-worthy sonnets, but we did create our own songs, poems, lab reports, and choreography to express the knowledge base we inherited, acquired, and constructed. I wanted to learn in her class. To this day, I remain warmed by her gentle yet insistent invitation to identify as a creator.

I wanted my students to experience something like what I had experienced with Ms. Jarvis because cultivating our creative muscle may be one of the most profound gifts we can give ourselves and others and one of the most ready sources of joy we can tap.

MY QUEST TO CREATE A JOYFUL CLASS

I have been on a quest to infuse joy into my teaching for a while now. My first conscious spark came when Carmen Johnston, a mentor on my tenure committee, said that teaching English should be fun for me (personal communication, September 13, 2012). She was not just attempting to alleviate my nerves as a newly hired, full-time faculty member. She was also previewing a foundational concept of transformational equity work: Perfectionism and the belief that success comes with excessive hours of work are tools of oppression, tools of manufacturing a hierarchy that disconnects the vast majority of humans from their personal empowerment, from their source of joy.

A few weeks after Carmen offered her advice, Dr. Cesar Cruz, a community educator, visited our campus to talk about how traditional schooling must be upended if we are going to draw out the strengths of Black and Brown men, a group historically underserved by our community college English courses. I felt particularly committed to adjusting my curriculum to better meet the needs of men of color because my course completion rates, like that of so many of my Language Arts colleagues, demonstrated that I had significant learning to do in this area.

In his talk, Dr. Cruz insisted that he'd never met anybody who liked being *schooled*. "But I've also never met anybody that doesn't like learning." He paused, letting that sink in (Cruz, 2012).

Schooling and learning are not the synonyms they seem. Schooling is about conformity and obedience, while learning ignites creativity and curiosity. Learning is what I had loved about Ms. Jarvis' class.

With this advice, I pieced together a theory about my teaching, a theory to counter the vast majority of my educational experiences. In short, humans are creators, and they derive joy and purpose through creation.

I have no problem advancing this theory when I teach creative writing. But for some reason, in composition courses, I am often sucked toward conformity, toward a type of schooling that wrings life out of my teaching and, worse, out of too many of my students' learning experiences. I attribute part of this challenge to the skills I feel obligated to teach as a composition instructor—students *have* to know what a thesis is—and part of this challenge to the fact that it can be difficult to tackle weighty social justice concepts, like the erasure of indigenous identity or environmental racism, with a light, playful touch.

Recently, it became clear that my struggle actually emanates from a pervasive deficit mindset: a mindset I must consistently watch for and resist because it reinforces conformity, not curiosity. It interferes with my ability to see that having fun can coexist alongside rigorous work.

When I shared my vow to center joy with colleagues, I often felt them bristle, even across a phone line. As the fall semester of 2021 kicked off, one of my composition colleagues doubted that fun could include challenge, doubted that this attitude could also cover course outline objectives.

I understood those doubts. I remember bristling in years past when the seemingly fluffy statement rolled off another instructor's tongue. I was skeptical of their intentions. Do they just want to be popular? Are they shying away from the hard content, leaving me to clean up what hasn't been taught? Didn't they risk insulting students by offering work that didn't respect the students' intellectual capacities?

Back then I was less clear that challenge can coexist with, even be the foundation of, joyful learning. Back then I hadn't realized that when I infuse fun into my curriculum, I also infuse flexibility—a key quality that allows instructors to meet students where they are and seek strategies to grow our minds together.

THE EVOLUTION OF JOY AND PLAY IN THE COMPOSITION CLASSROOM

In 2012, with Carmen and Dr. Cruz's advice at the forefront of my attention, my curriculum and pedagogy slowly morphed. My course materials and routines became more grounded in material I loved; my teaching practice slowly became more flexible. For example, I made time to play silly games at the start of class. I would try simple things like playing "Would you rather. . . ." Or I might ask students to post a pun, "You know, a dad joke," on the board. Both community builders translated well to the chat feature on Zoom.

Surprisingly, the more flexible I became, the more ideas I had about including play in the class. In fact, in March of 2020, just a week before rumblings of California's shelter-in-place orders, my students had been playing games that their classmates had invented as part of a research project.

We started the semester preparing to compose an essay about Andrea Smith's first three chapters of *Conquest: Sexual Violence and the American*

Indian Genocide (2015). To bring the urgency of her ideas to life and to add an element of synthesis into the paper, I crafted a project which asked students to team up and conduct independent research on a particular indigenous group's modern-day struggles. Each student team located research about their chosen indigenous community's cultural assets and current sociopolitical struggles. Then the teams designed a game to teach their classmates about their findings.

Our classroom took on the feel of a game night once the games were ready. We set up stations for student groups to rotate through. We had snacks for participants to munch on. In one corner, Jesus's team presented a 3-D puppet show about the Kiribati's struggles with plastic pollution and rising sea levels. Bridget's team designed a Jenga game with color-coded tiles representing different categories of facts about the Zapatistas. The biggest hit, designed by a team of female students, looked like a version of Chutes and Ladders. Players attempted to make their way home from a *maquiladora* (manufacturing plant) just outside of Juarez, Mexico. The game emphasized the struggles related to the ongoing femicide targeting the poorest women just across the U.S. border. Most of the maquiladora workers had migrated away from indigenous communities located in rural areas in the Mexican states of Oaxaca, Chiapas, and Guerrero.

Within this assignment, and particularly on this day, I had certainly managed to meld the ingredients of joy—creativity and a commitment to something larger—with meaty, social-justice related content. And, while the day was a success on the whole, as were the later research papers, I still recall walking away noticing the gaps, the deficits, the skills not yet mastered. Hadn't one group forgotten to cite their material in MLA 8 style sufficiently? Hadn't another group set up the game in a way that required far too much prior knowledge for players to make any meaningful guesses? How could I be sure that Oscar actually knew how to find information in our library databases? He'd been absent so often.

I even recall being upset with Oscar during the game session. His group was stationed at the whiteboard, hosting a version of Spin the Bottle. Oscar stepped into a leadership role, inventing adaptations to the rules when he noticed the game wasn't working. But all I could focus on that day was that Oscar had barely shown up to plan for his group's presentation.

In other words, on this day of purposeful play, I looked for what went wrong, for the deficiencies in the students' performances and in my own setup. In looking for what didn't work, I missed what mattered: Oscar had shown up to learn and to support his group. Oscar had cared enough to show off his leadership skills. I was the one who wasn't prepared to greet the talents, the assets he was choosing to show.

As I prepared future courses during the pandemic, I vowed to stop that joy-killing habit of focusing on what needs to be better. I vowed to center on what's good. I vowed to remember that amplifying joy is a path that leads to a love of learning.

SUBTLE SHIFTS PAY OFF

While I did make major shifts to the curriculum, it was the more subtle shifts that truly paid off. Indeed, I would argue that what had been missing pre-pandemic in my composition courses was the subtle shift to focus on students' assets, to remain flexible and responsive as individual students found their way through new content.

During the pandemic, in my composition courses, I made small shifts to my daily in-class rhythm, staking out more space for students to read, write, and share. I paused more to validate individual students' interpretations. Obviously, this wasn't so simple. Zoom discussions, even when they are about the topic of love, often feel slow and choppy. Still, I stuck with my intention and by the time we started our short story unit, most students eagerly volunteered responses.

One discussion was particularly lively. After we had reviewed a passage from our assigned story, I posed the question: "Does Junot Diaz's short story, "How to Date a Brown Girl," flip traditional expectations of any male archetypes? Consider details from the story as well as definitions of love offered by bell hooks."

Roxana responded first with an emphatic, "No." She pointed to a line where she claimed the narrator sounded "cocky and overly confident, just like a traditional *machista*."

"Interesting. Where does that cockiness come from?" I asked the class.

"He's not cocky. He's more insecure," Jesus volunteered. "It's like he takes an identity depending on the type of girl he meets. On page 149, he says, 'You'll wonder how she feels about Dominicans. Don't ask.' He tries to make himself the person he's not because he feels his race and background are not good enough. Not cool enough. Embarrassing."

"Jesus, you are making me think about how racism can affect our sense of self, can encourage us to hide parts of ourselves," I said.

The more I validated responses, the more students contributed.

Jesus added, "Most men would rather hold on to their ego than show a type of affection. Pride and ego matter to them more than anything. It's what they believe is being a man."

A few students added onto Jesus's comments, mostly agreeing with him, before I nudged the class to make connections to our earlier readings: "Do you all see any links between the narrator's desire to protect his ego and some of the definitions of love that bell hooks offered us?"

Isiah raised his virtual hand. "There's that quote on page 42 of *Honesty: Be True to Love* where bell hooks said, 'loving justice between a man and a woman does not stand a chance when other men's manhood matters more.' I think that fits."

As I offered an affirming finger snap to Isiah, Brenda's virtual hand popped up, signaling she was ready to break her silence. "I agree with Isiah.

It does seem like he cares more about other men and what they think," she said. "Notice that most of the instructions start with what the man should not do, opposed to what he should. It's almost like the narrator thinks there's masculinity in acting aloof."

A few more students commented, but I had an eye on the clock and needed to wrap the discussion. "I love how you are all building off of each other," I said. "These are interesting observations. Write them down. Capture the bling. Remember, you can use these ideas in your critical thinking posts, which are due tomorrow night." I switched my slides, projecting the work I wanted them to do before the next class, then continued, "It seems like many of you see Yunior's character as sort of reinforcing archetypal ideals of masculinity. But I wonder, do you think the story *as a whole* is also doing that? Do we, as readers, feel differently? Do we have any epiphanies or ah-ha moments? That's something to consider as you write."

By offering a more literary line of questioning, I hoped students would take a fresh look at the story when they wrote. Of course, I was also certain that many literary concepts were new for several students. Few had considered that a reader—not a character—might have an epiphany. I figured that I could continue to introduce this concept as I responded to their low-stakes critical thinking posts, short writing assignments that served as a stepping-stone or early draft for an upcoming essay.

I have used low-stakes writing prompts to replace traditional plot-driven quizzes for years, but the way I responded to writing shifted during the pandemic. With a focus on joy, I decided that my comments should mirror the type of response I gave to my creative writing students.

In creative writing classes, we follow a simple writing group ritual of Bless (name something strong, something that works in your peer's writing) and Press (ask questions to clarify or elaborate). Students Bless and Press both with in-class quick writes and with more polished pieces written by their peers. I always pause, right after students experience the ritual for the first time, to ask how it feels to have their work blessed and pressed in this way. Students consistently echo Elizabeth's comment: "We don't usually talk about what works in other writing classes. This is so nice. I like getting that kind of feedback."

When I integrated the Bless and Press ritual into my composition course, I noticed how it positioned me as one reader, not the ultimate authority. Students could decide whether to answer the questions I posed when they developed the draft into a longer piece. The ritual fit smoothly into all stages of the writing process from peer review to teacher comments on major essays. Students even blessed and pressed their final drafts, as a sort of author's note for me to reply to.

To illustrate, after the class discussion about "How to Date a Brown Girl," students continued to wrestle with notions of love and masculinity in their Critical Thinking Posts. Roxana doubled down on her belief that Yunior was not flipping any archetypal scripts, even if he wanted to on some level. I blessed her ideas, with the following comment:

> Roxana, I appreciate the way you notice the tone shifts in the story. In your passage below, you make a strong point that Yunior's insight only lasts briefly before his insecurity actually pushes him toward male dominance. You wrote: "Yunior mentions to 'tell her that you love her skin, her lips, because, in truth, you love them more than you love your own' (Diaz, 147). Something about the tone he says it in feels as if Yunior let his guard down for a quick second before switching the topic back to seem macho once again. It feels as if for a split second, Yunior wanted to slip in how he feels insecure about his own personality or features, and that's why he wants to be more manly; he believes that dominance can make up for the things he's insecure about."

Earlier in her post, Roxana exposed how Yunior's character was bound to traditional macho roles. She wrote:

> Yunior also mentions that you should '. . . never lose a fight on a first date or that will be the end of it' (Diaz, 146). He's trying to show his dominance and fight for his side, rather than to talk things out with his partner. He'd rather argue for his side, rather than talking things out and figuring out a better way to settle the problem. This reminds me of a quote in *All About Love* that states 'loving justice between a man and a woman does not stand a chance when other men's manhood matters more' (hooks, 42). Both quotes connect because it defines how you can't have a relationship, if the only thing that matters is the guy winning, or the guy trying to show off that he can fight back, or just show his dominance in general. There also can't be a relationship if there's no communication, no respect, and no trust. In a way, some people want to have a relationship but not put in the effort; it's mostly just because they want to be seen in one, or to just have someone there, but the love isn't actually real.

To press Roxana's thinking in terms of literary analysis, I typed the following series of questions:

> Clearly you see the main character as stuck in traditional roles of masculinity. So, do you think the *author* is telling this story to expose men like Yunior and their struggles? Like is the reader supposed to feel sorry for Yunior? Or feel like Yunior is a jerk and he needs to be shamed? I ask because I wonder if you think readers, like you and your classmates, have any ah-ha's about the way gender stereotypes get reinforced, even though Yunior does not.

A week or so later, as Roxana wrote her literary analysis essay for our short story unit, she had the opportunity to address those questions or to explore a new line of thinking. For the most part, she chose to ignore my question about the reader's epiphany. Instead, she built up an argument about the symbolism in the two stories she analyzed. I was pleased to see that shift, given we had also spent several classes digging into symbolism and the way it connected to Chicana female archetypes like *La Llorona* and *La Malinche*. Her overall analysis of the two stories was outstanding, but what I found most affirming was a comment from her self-reflection. She wrote:

> In all honesty, I felt like it was easy for me to write this essay because I had talked about the writings in class and in breakout rooms so it was easier for me to jot my ideas down since I already had a few in mind. Also, I feel more proud of this essay more than my last one because I feel like there's no forced writing in this one, it was all smooth and thought out and it was actually pretty fun to write. Usually, I would get stuck on how to bring in a quote or how to blend it in and then talk about it, but for this essay it was mostly like once I started writing, I couldn't stop.

My effort to validate students' assets enlivened the learning environment for Roxana. It also made my time spent reading student writing more joyful. Figuring out how to celebrate what was good motivated me to read students' weekly posts. Figuring out how to ask an authentic question that might stoke a student's natural instinct to investigate the world was actually fun. Students and I felt as though we were in a conversation as respectful intellectuals.

Pre-pandemic, I rarely approached a class with such a steady goal of naming and amplifying what is good. In the past, I would sabotage the joy by anxiously trying to fill up any perceived gaps in required skills, as if students should have already mastered them.

The pandemic sparked a much-needed breakthrough: I finally internalized how centering joy within learning spaces is a radical act. It is a counterweight to the way higher education is steeped in deficit perspectives about students' capabilities—and by extension, about a teacher's ability to be both rigorous and joyful, a warm demander, as Zaretta Hammond (2015) might say, an alliance builder who partners with learners to support their natural talents and cultivate their life's purpose.

My breakthrough revealed to me how centering joy is an asset-based approach to classroom instruction, a way to celebrate and amplify the linguistic, navigational, familial, and aspirational wealth that students from historically marginalized groups possess (Yosso, 2005).

When I sustain a focus on centering joy, I am also implementing a trauma-informed approach to instructional design (Baez et al., 2020; Davidson, 2017), allowing laughter and natural curiosity to heal the wounds of traditional academia's overly assimilative process, a process that favors objectivity and competition, a process that cultivates fear. In *Teaching Community*, bell hooks notes that "the culture of fear that is rampant on most college campuses . . .

undermines the capacity of students to learn. Fear-based students doubt that they can accomplish what they need to accomplish" (2003, p. 132). I must add that as teachers, when we are driven by fear, we doubt our capacity to engage all students. We shut down our ability to uplift the unique assets of individual students whose creative ideas may break new ground in our fields.

As my breakthrough took hold, I vowed to work harder to notice what was good in students' work. I committed to validating students' written responses, and in doing so, I saw that students began to trust that my actions matched my stated values; they began to shed their fear of saying the wrong thing, and they began to take on creator identities, much like I took on a creator identity in Ms. Jarvis's class.

MORE TALENT ON DISPLAY

When students are invited to express creativity, they are free to show us even more of their talents, amplifying joy all around.

For the final unit in our composition course, we focused on Luis Valdez's satirical one-acts from *Teatro Campesino*, a theater company launched during the Chicano Movement. In addition to writing a literary analysis paper about Valdez's plays, I asked students to work in pairs to design an original satire.

I gave students choice in terms of the genre of the satire: They could present a video modeled after the *Key & Peele* sketch "TeachingCenter" (2015), draw a poster/cartoon strip similar to artist Esther Hernandez's *Sun Mad Raisins* (1982), or a write a piece like a play or an article typically found in *McSweeney's*.

Two of the steadiest participants in the class created a biting satirical video parodying a pharmaceutical advertisement. They advertised *Gay Away*, a pill to "cure" homosexuality, and highlighted the side effects such as "increased suicidal ideation" and "loss of fashion sense."

Andrew, a young man who barely participated in my Zoom sessions but who did his best to submit all writing assignments despite working long hours to contribute to his household, shined in this project. He submitted a satirical video using stop-motion animation. It featured his siblings, their rubber duckies and frogs, and an elaborate stage that spanned the dining table. Along the edge of the stage, Andrew simulated a sidewalk with cardboard strips and placed two toy soldiers, the kind whose rifles are ready to shoot, on patrol along the sidewalk, as if they were overseeing the ocean front.

Just off the sidewalk, a whale can be seen floating among plastic wrap as the soldiers, narrated by Andrew and his brother, talk about how helpful their inventions have been for the world and how profitable they've been for their families. Moments later, we hear his sister, playing an ocean animal, say, deadpan, "Yes, all the animals are so excited about the new play structure you have built for them!" The camera returns to the whale who is now entangled among a series of pink and green plastic straws. The image high-lights the incongruity in the statement. As the piece carries on, the animals express appreciation, in unison, as if children saluting the flag, for "all the wonderful inventions the soldiers have brought to the world." The absurdity grows as the piece force us to think about the ethics behind our inventions.

Within this final project, Andrew demonstrated his depth of understand-ing of satirical devices while also showing off his talent with script writing and stop-motion animation, all assets I had little idea he possessed. What's more, his love of learning spread beyond my classroom to engage his siblings in the joy of thinking and creating together. It felt like a Ms. Jarvis moment.

He reminded me that a vow to center joy and teach what I love is im-portant because it undoes the destructive nature of schooling that tends to exclude so many first-generation students on my campus. Rather than insist on conformity and obedience, I centered learning and play. Rather than as-suming I have gaps in skills to fill, I pushed myself to validate the multiple ways of knowing and communicating that students already possess. Those changes in my practice made all the difference.

My vow, one I hope to recommit to each semester, pushes me to look for what's good, to amplify that, and to invite students to expand on what matters to them, to grow their own curiosity, to grow their creativity, to remember that teaching and learning should be fun.

CONCLUSION

My breakthrough emerged after serious reflection on Ms. Jarvis's 4th-grade classroom, which remains, unequivocally, the most joyful and transforma-tive learning experience I have had. In her classroom, Ms. Jarvis fostered a desire to learn and take risks. She nurtured a community of students who celebrated one another's curiosity and creativity. The more consistently I emulate her approach, the more I notice my community college students not just persist in my composition courses but flourish. They bond with one another more readily, they take risks with written and oral interpretations, they demonstrate more curiosity, creativity, and vulnerability. They are en-gaged in learning right through the end of the 18-week course because they feel more relaxed as learners.

Elementary school educators like Ms. Jarvis understand, perhaps intui-tively, the benefits of play and joy. Why, then, was it so difficult for me, as an instructor in higher education, to fully embrace this approach? Why did it take the pandemic's collective trauma to unleash my commitment to joy?

In writing this piece, I had to grapple with my resistance to centering joy. Institutional and peer expectations about "standards" and rigor cer-tainly played a significant role. Another factor was the sheer time needed to reimagine my social justice content while making room for play. But my primary block turned out to be the nagging fear that I might not be adding value to my students' skill sets.

Ironically, educational research (Forbes, 2021) and my own observations demonstrate that student engagement and learning are amplified when instructors center joy. Being aware of my subtle forms of resistance has made it far easier to sustain my commitment. Each semester, as I plan a new class, I ask myself a few key questions: What happens when I use joy as a grounding mechanism from which to plan curriculum, to adjust assessment, and to modify day-to-day lessons? How do students like Andrew, Roxana, and Isiah respond to assignments that invite play? What strengths and talents are my students showing me they possess?

I invite other community college composition colleagues to join me in this radical practice of centering joy. May we shed our own fears and notice how doing so amplifies our students' assets and fosters an environment where all of us, teachers and students, move toward our unique purpose on this Earth.

RECOMMENDED READING

Forbes, L. (2021). The process of play in learning in higher education: A phenomenological study. *Journal of Teaching and Learning, 15*(1), 57–73. https://.doi .org/10.22329/jtl.v15i1.6515

> A comprehensive study that exposes why play (and joy) are so rare in higher education and demonstrates the myriad benefits of student learning when instructors do commit to a playful curriculum.

Hammond, Z. (2015). *Culturally responsive teaching and the brain: Promoting authentic engagement and rigor among culturally and linguistically diverse students.* Corwin.

> An in-depth book that explains the neuroscience of asset-based instructional practices and provides tangible ideas for joyful instructional design.

hooks, b. (2003). *Teaching community: A pedagogy of hope.* (pp. 127–137). Routledge.

> A brief article that emphasizes the transformative learning that is possible when we teach with love and joy in higher education.

Muhammad, G. (2023). *Unearthing joy: A guide to culturally and historically responsive curriculum and instruction.* Scholastic.

> A framework and practical guide demonstrating how joy is rooted in the cultural and historical realities of Black students. Lesson plans explain how to cultivate joy and enhance students' criticality.

About Chapter 6

Like teachers across the country, **Lisa Orta** faces a crunch time when her community college shuts down due to the pandemic. She and her colleagues have one weekend to shift from in-person teaching to working remotely, from whiteboards to screen sharing, from fresh faces to no faces. "My colleagues and I began a journey that forever changed us. . . . All that we learned and made has a shelf-life way beyond remote instruction."

As someone who knows the technology ropes better than most, Orta becomes one of the key trainers, a role she takes to heart. But it is the inevitable snags during a crisis that give Orta her breakthrough: the key to learning new things is working collegially. As her teammate and leader, Anne Kingsley, explains: "Peer-based leadership is important, essential, in and outside of a pandemic. . . . When we witness each other's strengths, losses, vulnerabilities, and creativity, we become closer, we learn from each other" (Kingsley & Orta, 2022).

CHAPTER 6

Trainer/Collaborator/Coach

Helping Faculty Navigate the Pandemic Pivot to Remote Instruction

Lisa Orta

The abrupt transition to remote instruction in March 2020 due to the COVID-19 shutdown required instructors at my California community college to hit the reset button on a dime. The story I tell here is a keyhole view of what that transition looked like from the vantage point of a front-line worker. Admittedly, I focus mainly on the positive, the insights and growth gained from the intimacy I shared with a relative handful of instructors. I don't write much here about the tears and frustration, the anger and despair—there was plenty of that. I don't write much here about my feelings of exhaustion and isolation—there was plenty of that too. I was lucky enough to be part of a strong faculty-led team whose mission was to keep the boat afloat. I was lucky enough to possess a skill set that allowed me to help steer the course.

The shutdown showed instructors that there are ways to leverage technology that benefit everyone engaged in the teaching and learning process. The Information Technology (IT) function at most colleges like ours does not provide instructional design support for online pedagogy. That function is left up to Distance Education (DE), which at our college is led by faculty. In transitioning to the remote modality, instructors were given peer-based opportunities to reexamine their course design and delivery with a fresh pair of eyes. Many now have more accessible and equitable course materials. Many offer courses that have a stronger focus on course learning objectives and authentic assessment. All of us, whether teaching in online, hybrid, or on-site modalities, or delivering instructional support, now have new tools in our toolboxes.

The pedagogical lessons I identify in this essay are ones that stayed with us beyond the chaos and setbacks of the shutdown: each learner comes to the table with unique goals and an individual capacity to learn; context is everything; it isn't the lesson plan that drives the lesson, it's the learner's engagement that gives the lesson value; listening and observing should upstage directing and urgency; there is joy in the process. This is my story of how one member of the DE team at our college found her sea legs in the midst of a storm.

March 13, 2020, Friday the 13th—the day my grandfather used to say, with a twinkle in his eye, was his lucky day—was the last day we gathered together on campus. In response to the COVID-19 pandemic, our college was shutting down the following Monday, March 16. In a 3-day turn-around, all classes were going remote. I remember that Friday for its dark, eerie undertone of fear, uncertainty, and controlled panic. I also remember a bright, optimistic overtone of calm, competence, and collegiality. I can still hear the voice of our DE coordinator, Anne Kingsley, broadcast over a makeshift microphone she found in a classroom closet and hooked up to the mounted speakers: "We've got this. We will help you learn what you need to know. We will get through this together."

Our DE team, led by Anne, sprang to action, setting an agenda for work-shops on the basics of digital literacy, Canvas (our learning management system), and Zoom. The hallways began to swell with overflow. Someone found a way to open additional classrooms and bathrooms to accommodate the growing number of instructors needing training. Anne quickly mobi-lized Training Leads—instructors historically involved with various aspects of distance learning—to provide one-to-one and small-group support for instructors who were struggling with any aspect of the pivot to remote in-struction, which was basically everyone in the building.

I wound my way through the crowd to the front of the room where Anne was posting the day's training schedule and locations on the whiteboard and asked, "What can I do to help?"

"You are a Training Lead," she answered over her shoulder, "get started."

All of the emotions associated with imposter syndrome washed over me. As experienced as I was with online instruction, it would have never occurred to me that I had the knowledge and capacity to help instructors of various disciplines and skill levels with the breadth and depth of questions they might have in this chaotic and frantic moment. These were colleagues for whom I have deep respect and loyalty—what if I gave someone incorrect information or faulty advice? But one glance around the room told me this was triage, a go-with-what-you-know moment, and it was my responsibility to take my place.

I spotted a psychology professor I've known for more than 25 years, a colleague I've gone to now and then for sage and friendly therapeutic ad-vice. He was pale and disoriented. His hands were shaking. His eyes were squinting at his laptop screen. Not too long ago, this instructor could be seen hauling his personal overhead projector across campus, a well-worn leather briefcase filled with transparency slides slung over his shoulder. Motivated to lessen the physical burden of the projector and slides, he had recently converted his transparencies to Powerpoints, and learned how to use classroom computers to project them during lectures. The sudden pivot to remote instruction required him to make an even larger leap: He now needed to make voiceover videos of his Powerpoints. I sat down next to him and with a reassuring hand on his arm I promised that based on his success with his Powerpoints, we could get him ready for Monday.

I showed him some voiceover videos I recently made. His eyes widened, he took a deep breath, and with a hint of a smile he set up his screen to record his first video. Promising to check back later, I moved on to another instructor who needed my attention and support. There were so many I helped that day—a former student who now taught health science at our satellite campus, English instructors, ESL instructors, math instructors, business instructors, language instructors.

Classroom teachers were suddenly required to learn a whole new way of doing things on an impossibly short timeline. Our team helped instructors with the technical aspect of remote instruction, but mostly we worked to translate chaos into order, to reassure instructors that they would get the help necessary to navigate in, what were for most of them, uncharted waters.

By Monday, Anne had created a multipronged approach for instructor support. One of these prongs was one-to-one training. She emailed a weekly sign-up grid to all faculty. Training leads listed their areas of expertise, instructors completed the sentence frame: "I need help with . . . ," and pairings were made. Working on the Call Center, as I came to characterize it, blurred the division between our public and private lives in profound ways. Here's a snapshot of some things I learned from March to May:

- *People are very invested in your liking their cats.* Many many cats jumped and slunk into view in those early days. I'm a dog person, not a cat person, so it was a stretch, but I quickly learned that cat commentary was a powerful icebreaker.
- *It is human nature to blame the messenger.* Panicked and scared, instructors expected me to have answers to questions I had myself. "When will it be safe to return to campus?" "What precautions will be taken?" I am not an immunologist. I am not the chancellor of our district. I am not a soothsayer. The last thing they wanted to hear was the only answer I had to give them: "I don't know."
- *In a crisis, people lose their sense of humor, their awareness of time, and the need to self-censor.* My jokes fell flat. Instructors were late to our Zoom appointments. Cameras were sometimes aimed at body parts and domestic environments that might have been better kept private from my view.
- *In a shut-down, people are lonely.* Instructors come to campus and interact with students and colleagues as a regular part of their day. Working remotely was massively unfamiliar to them. Sometimes my job was to be a better listener than a trainer.

WORKING IN A CALL CENTER IS CHALLENGING

In the beginning, each Zoom meeting was a wild card. It was like reliving the first day of school every hour on the hour. I didn't know what the instructors knew and didn't know about technology or online pedagogy. I didn't know what the instructors valued and prioritized about teaching and learning. And asking instructors to screen share their online courses felt a bit like asking them to show me their underwear drawers—for different reasons, we were often mutually uncomfortable. Over time I developed an informal diagnostic that helped establish a starting point. Regardless of the question that brought instructors to my screen, I flashed my well-worn teacher's smile, kept my tone friendly and even, and said "Let's take a quick look at your course." When I saw something that needed immediate fixing, I'd say, "Do me a favor and click on . . ." These tactics, combined with lots of strong coffee, saw me through those first few months.

SPOILER ALERT: I DON'T SEE MYSELF AS A TRAINER ANYMORE

After four semesters of remote instruction, my takeaways are more panoramic. There were times I made missteps, times I was overwhelmed, times I felt I was doing the best work of my career. As I gathered more confidence and perspective, my understanding of my role shifted. Not unlike what happened when I picked myself up off the floor after my first year of classroom teaching 34 years ago, my task was to shed the role of enabler and don the role of catalyst. The snapshots that follow trace my transformation from trainer to collaborator.

THE PEDAGOGICAL IS PERSONAL

One of the first instructors I worked with was returning to the college post-retirement to teach Critical Thinking: Writing About Literature. She was caught off-guard when classes were pivoted to remote instruction. At our first session, rooted in my "fix-it" mode, I suggested she map out the six instructional weeks for the course, divide those weeks into units, and then create learning modules for presenting course materials, student-to-instructor and student-to-student interaction, and assessments. But what she wanted to show me was a series of fine art images she had curated and embedded onto Canvas pages.

She urgently wanted my feedback on how well these images related to the literary content of her course. I wanted our time together to be focused on course design. Embedded graphics, right out of the chute, struck me as unnecessary.

This conflict persisted throughout our weekly sessions. I stuck with the technical design features. She pushed back, wanting to translate a deeply personal approach to the subject matter to her online class. Once the graphics, which I need to say were stunning and extraordinary, were embedded and sequenced to her satisfaction, she insisted with the same intensity that I listen to her read the narrative of her instructional text aloud. Her jaw set tight, she leaned forward and filled the screen with her face as she read. Tension continued to build between us and at one point in the process she stopped signing up for my help.

EACH INSTRUCTOR COMES TO REMOTE INSTRUCTION THROUGH THEIR OWN DOOR

Where did I go wrong with this instructor? As a trainer, I expected our time together to be focused on the "how" of getting her course designed and student-ready. If I had taken a collaborator role and began our work together through a "why" lens, I would have considered why the graphics were the vertebrae of her course design, for example, her pairing of Kate Chopin's "The Story of an Hour" with René Magritte's *The Lovers*. This would have led me to understand why reading her instructional narrative aloud to me was so crucial to her.

She did try to invite me into her teaching space, and I squandered that invitation. Lesson learned. As a collaborator, I am not inviting instructors into my house, they are inviting me into theirs. I am a guest and need to mind my manners.

REVERSE COURSE DESIGN GIVES ONLINE COURSE ITS FOUNDATION

Another English instructor I worked with had no online teaching experience. She had taught first-year college writing and reading for many years, but now she was scattered and panicked. Each time I met with her, her head was in a different quadrant of the screen, sometimes not visible at all. She knew she didn't have the digital literacy necessary, so she was beginning to rely on her adult son for help. That scenario was clearly not sustainable— her son was not an educator, nor was he the instructor of record.

To focus and calm her, I began our work together with the question, "How is it going for your students?" She described ways they were struggling with pandemic-related challenges, and ways an assignment she had spontaneously given them based on a COVID-19 related reading from *The Atlantic* seemed to help them process their experiences. She was eager to read student work aloud to me, which, this time, I listened to. To frame how to go forward, I then guided her through making an instructional page that listed the learning objectives for the course. At our second meeting, each time she described a student activity or read a student response, I related the content back to a learning objective on that page. By our third session, she began to frame reports of student progress in the context of learning objectives, and soon she was proactively building instructional units with learning objectives at the center. Once we shifted our focus to her students and to her learning objectives, this instructor's panic calmed, and her course design no longer felt like random chaos.

COLLABORATION IS CONTAGIOUS

As she became more confident in her course design, this instructor began to collaborate with her students by encouraging them to bring readings into the course. While she and I set up interactive activities, her students contributed to a learning community that helped them navigate, together, through a troubled time. At a moment in human history when we were all feeling powerless and uncertain, she and her students built what I call a "Forever Class," the one we recall many years later for its gift of comfort, inspiration, and meaning.

TECHNOLOGY SERVES CONTENT, NOT THE OTHER WAY AROUND

While technology often presents itself as a panacea, it is merely a tool that gets its value from its user. At each of our initial sessions this instructor would ask about tools or platforms she believed would magically fix the shortcomings of her course—Padlet, Pronto, Kahoot, and so many others. Aware that learning how to set up learning modules and make instructional pages in Canvas was enough of a technical challenge for her, I stalled conversations about these tools until we had the flow of her course pinned to a clear destination.

Once her course took shape, and her interest in collaborating with her students emerged as a central value, I took a chance with Hypothesis, a social annotation platform. This tool matched her intention to give students a place to share readings and discuss their "markings" in a digital learning space. She learned how to use it in a snap, and, to my relief, she left her yearning for all other tempting technology in the ether.

THERE IS ALWAYS ROOM FOR IMPROVEMENT

Another instructor I worked with was extremely organized and deliberate in her course presentation. This instructor had done a tremendous amount of work moving two ESL classes online—Beginning Oral Communication

Skills and Integrated Academic Reading, Writing, and Study Skills—all while she was at home with remote-learning teenagers and a new puppy. There were continual interruptions during our sessions, but she consistently returned to the screen keenly focused on where we left off.

As we worked together, she hinted that she wanted to "up" the look of her instructional pages and the functionality of her course overall. She asked for a tour of one of my courses. I shared my screen. She noticed the strengths of my course design: a consistent visual and design strategy, embedded media, placement of tutorials, opportunities to inspire further learning. She asked if we could make her class look like mine. Instinct told me rather than jumping into the "how," we needed to step back and consider the "why."

AUDIENCE IS EVERYTHING

My father, an engineer, would come home after a long day of work and ask us at the dinner table why no one seemed to consider the end user. When I was 10 years old, that was a difficult question to answer, but now, channeling that question, the answer to how best to work with this instructor became clear.

We moved back to her screen, and I prompted her to click on Student View, a setting that shows the instructor exactly what a student sees in a course. My course was an advanced critical thinking course, hers beginning ESL courses—very different student demographics, very different learning needs. "You are a student in this class," I told her. "What do you see? What is clear and easy to follow?" I asked. "What is confusing?" and, "What more could you offer?" This set the tone for our many weeks of work together. We'd move to Student View, take note of ways the course design was directing the student experience, jump back to the Teacher View and work to make changes. We combined her knowledge of ESL instruction with my knowledge of behind-the-curtain strategies to arrive at a collaboration that was student-centered.

TEACHING IS LEARNING

I first met this next instructor in May 2020. She was preparing her summer Principles and Practices of Early Childhood Education class. She had team-taught an online course in spring, but this would be her first time flying solo in the virtual world. She also faced the challenge of teaching highly interactive activities—puppet play, music and movement, storytelling—online to students who would turn around and use them in "live" interactions with children. And the start date for summer school was right around the corner.

I suggested we begin by looking at the course she team-taught with another instructor. She wanted to begin by showing me where she stored her files and then struggled a bit to find them. We were starting at ground zero.

This instructor went from zero to ten in her understanding of online pedagogy in a matter of months. I attribute the rate of her progress to her deep understanding of scaffolded learning, something intrinsic in her field. She also had the ability to metacognitively apply what she knew about learning theory to her own experience as a learner. She signed up to work with me at the same time, on the same day, each week. She told me, "My whole family knows you. When I write LISA TIME on our kitchen white board, they know not to interrupt me *for any reason* during our sessions." She never hesitated to say, "I don't remember how to do that," or, "Let me take a moment and write down some notes." Her comfort with her learning style set the pace for our collaboration.

Over the course of our time together, I became a grandmother for the first time. "When you hold him," she advised, "establish eye contact and let him invite you into his space. Soon enough," she added, "he will start to imitate you." Citing several early childhood theorists, she then emphasized, "It's all about the importance of play." And with that she framed what delighted me about our work together. There was an invitation, there was mutual respect, there was a shared professional standard, and there was a lot of what I call "teacher-nerd" fun.

THE PRINCIPLES OF TEACHING AND LEARNING ARE UNIVERSAL

Because online pedagogy is rooted in strong principles of teaching and learning, DE Training Leads were able to collaborate with instructors of various technical skill levels and across disciplines. Now that I've observed close to 100 virtual classrooms, I know that helping a business instructor and an American Sign Language instructor create authentic assessments requires the same skills. Instructors know what mastery looks like; my job is to suggest strategies for scaffolding lessons, tools for measurement, and guiding language to facilitate student learning.

Other panoramic takeaways:

- *Instructors are people, and people amaze you.* The remote solutions lab that activity and studio instructors devised—printmaking kits, kitchen lab kits, phones mounted strategically as cameras, animated demonstrations, and so many more—were astounding and inspiring.
- *For many, good enough is truly good enough.* Instructors were doing all they could to stay calm and do their best. Doing their best had to be the standard.

- *The heart and soul of an online course is way more palpable to students than technically sophisticated design*—just ask them about their pandemic Forever Classes.
- *Less is more. Almost always.*
- *Continuous improvement is the language of love.*

My grandpa was right. Friday, March 13, 2020, was a very lucky day. My colleagues and I began a journey that forever changed us. As separated as we became physically from each other and from our students in the virtual worlds of Canvas and Zoom, as Anne predicted, we got through this together, and that goal continues to sustain us. We catapulted our collective technical literacy to a whole new level. And all that we learned and made has a shelf life way beyond remote instruction. The way learning a new language fosters empathy and insight for what is not yet known, leveraging technology as a tool for instruction has put us on the road to unexpected pedagogical destinations. Did my imposter syndrome dissolve once I understood my role as DE support? No. It sits on my shoulder to this day, but more lightly now that my response to the question "how?" is most often "why?"

CONCLUSION

In reflecting on the teacher training and collaborating I did during the shutdown, and taking the time to write about it, I was reminded that strong teachers hit the reset button all the time. The lessons we learn are embedded in the stories we tell, and the most powerful lessons may shift context but deserve repeating. Instructors and students are forever changed by what we learned during the shutdown about technology, about school, and about ourselves as learners. I don't want that thread to break. We each need to tell our stories to remind us of our resilience and our capacity to learn new things. I predict that at the core of our stories will be the reminder that hitting the reset button can bring us back to what we know to be essential and true.

RECOMMENDED READING

Flanagan, N. (2020). *Nora Flanagan: What COVID-19 revealed about US schools—and 4 ways to rethink education | TED Talk*. TEDx. https://www.ted.com/talks/nora_flanagan_what_covid_19_revealed_about_us_schools_and_4_ways_to_rethink_education

Chicago secondary school educator, Nora Flanagan, reflects on ways teaching through the pandemic deepened her understanding of students' lives. She articulates ways schools can reinvent themselves postpandemic to meet students' needs: engage parents, demand equity, support the whole student, and rethink assessment.

Kingsley A., & Orta, L. (2022, March 23). *Lifelines: Layered Voices in the Pivot to Online Instruction* [Faculty Lecture]. Diablo Valley College, Pleasant Hill, CA, USA. https://www.dvc.edu/about/governance/faculty-senate/lifelines.html

> This faculty lecture is an experimental layering of faculty voices and memory to explore the life-changing moment that grabbed our lives in March 2020. It illustrates how peer-based training and collaboration created lifelines of professional and personal support that sustained the continuity of the classroom and each other.

Ofgang, E. (2021, September 9). 4 lessons from remote learning. *TechLearning-Magazine*. https://www.techlearning.com/how-to/4-lessons-from-remote-learning

> Ofgang lists four soft skills which Ericka Mabion, iSpark PLTW/CTE coordinator at Kansas City Public Schools, believes students gained while learning remotely: more opportunities to connect, quick and seamless feedback from students and educators, opportunity for audio and video feedback and submissions, and deepened empathy among educators, students, and parents.

Thompson, M. (2020, December 9). Are We Teaching in a New World?: Yahdon Israel on Language Barriers, Educational Politics, and Online Teaching. *Teachers & Writers Magazine*. https://teachersandwritersmagazine.org/are-we-teaching-in-a-new-world-yahdon-israel-on-language-barriers-educational-politics-and-online-teaching/

> Thompson interviews Yahdon Israel, producer of the Language Barrier lecture series (IG TV) who encourages educators to engage with technology and to be transparent about learning how to best use it along with students. This shared experience, he says, is where the real learning begins.

About Chapter 7

When it comes to teaching English learners, personal experience pays off big time. Veteran high school teacher **Beth Daly** is faced with the daunting task of learning Romanian when she enters the Peace Corps in Moldova. The experience turns out to be a painful reminder that stumbling around looking for the right word or phrase is not simply a drain on the brain; it's a process "fraught with emotions" (Swain, 2013, p. 198). As Daly discovers, those emotions can stop us in our tracks. "When we are unable to communicate clearly, we can feel unseen, unknown, invisible," she explains.

The significance of Daly's breakthrough: emotions are too often overlooked as a key player in language acquisition. "Emotions are like 'the elephant in the room,'" according to Swain (2013, p. 195). Daly's high school students—who experience daily the emotional rollercoaster of learning English—become the beneficiaries of her revised approach to addressing issues of language and identity.

CHAPTER 7

Lessons From Moldova
From Language Learner to Language Teacher

Beth Daly

It was a late afternoon in September 2015, and I had been in Moldova for nearly four months. I climbed up the three flights of crumbling stairs in the dimly lit stairwell of Nadia's cinder block apartment building. I knocked on the door and Nadia greeted me, and then ushered me back to her son's bedroom, which doubled as her office space when she was tutoring me in Romanian. As Nadia gathered her materials, I stared out the window at the children swinging on the rusted playground equipment in the yard below. Nadia sat down across from me and, as we reviewed the lesson from a few days before, my chest started to tighten. I had been studying Romanian intensely since June and was currently surrounded by Romanian speakers at home and at work, and yet I felt like my brain was failing me. Nadia asked if I understood what I had done wrong on the homework assignment, and I lost it. Whatever *it* was. Tears began rolling down my face. I couldn't seem to understand the difference between what I had done and what was "correct," and my frustration felt paralyzing. I was horrified that I was 50 years old, and my emotions had hijacked my brain, and this realization made me cry even more. All the emotions of the day came rushing back to me: the interactions I had that morning with two of my partner teachers, the miscommunication with my host family about what time I would be leaving for school, the students who didn't understand my limited speaking skills. I felt defeated and useless and overwhelmed by my inability to communicate. I just wanted to be understood.

I was in that tiny Moldovan apartment because a year earlier, at the start of my 15th year of teaching, I knew that I needed to try something new. I had been teaching at the same school in the San Francisco Bay Area for my entire teaching career, and although I loved my students and adored my colleagues, I was burnt out. I was teaching 11th grade English and drama, putting on our school's Poetry Slam, and directing two student productions each year, and after 15 years of this I needed a change. I didn't want to leave teaching, but I needed some kind of sabbatical; I needed to recharge my teaching spark. So I did what any other 50-year-old would do: I joined the Peace Corps.

As an English Education volunteer in the Peace Corps, I would be able to deepen my teaching practice while challenging myself in new ways. I could take a leave of absence from my current teaching position, knowing that I would have a job in my school district when I returned. I wasn't a stranger to living in another culture; I had spent a year of high school as an exchange student in Japan and a year of college at the University of Iceland. But adapting to a new culture as an adult was a different type of challenge.

I was assigned to serve in Moldova, a former Soviet Republic located between Romania and Ukraine. By many estimates, Moldova is one of the poorest countries in Europe, and it is a country sharply divided over whether to align itself more closely with Russia or with the European Union (particularly Romania, which Moldova was once a part of). During our preservice training we were given intensive language classes in Romanian, and we stayed with Moldovan host families near the capital city, Chisinau. After 6 weeks of training, we were sent to our permanent site placements, which for me was Soroca, a small city in northern Moldova right on the border with Ukraine.

In that tiny Moldovan apartment, I was humbled to become a student again. I knew that I would be learning Romanian, but I was not fully prepared for how difficult language learning could be as an adult. The sponge that my brain had been when I was in high school and college—the brain that picked up languages easily and effortlessly— was suddenly a rock. I could sense what I wanted to learn, and I knew how I wanted the language to flow, but I felt stymied in all my efforts. I was stuck.

There are times as a teacher when I try to point out something that seems obvious to me, and when I ask a student if they understand, they respond with a look of complete bewilderment and frustration. It can be easy to overlook the emotions students experience in this moment, and to just try to "teach harder"—give them more information and alternate views in an effort to bridge the knowledge gap. And maybe that works sometimes. But most of the time, we need something different.

When I began crying, Nadia didn't continue to teach. She stopped the lesson and asked about my day. I walked her through the past few hours of the cultural and communication missteps: the male teacher who always seemed to lecture at me whenever we met to lesson plan and who ignored my recommendations, the other teacher who wanted to test students on material that the students hadn't studied (but which she thought they should already know), the overwhelming feeling I had when my brain was flooded with language I could barely understand, the distress I felt when I couldn't easily produce the sentences or ideas I wanted to produce, my exhaustion with the constant friction of trying to translate my thoughts into another language.

Just acknowledging the challenges I was facing helped to clear my brain for learning new material. It was almost like erasing the chalkboard of my brain—my brain was cluttered with all the emotions of the past few months, and I needed to let those feelings go before I could take in any new information. I wasn't suddenly fluent in Romanian, but it felt like I had created a clean slate for new material. And we moved forward. *Hai, mergem!* (Let's go!)

Back in my California classroom, I try to remember all these feelings, especially when dealing with language learners. The frustration of not being understood can deeply shape our interactions with others, especially when those others hold a position of authority over us. We can't understand a concept until we have language for that concept, and the process of learning that language can have a deeply emotional context. Language learners need to gain confidence with the words, and that confidence is being built on shaky ground at the beginning of the process. Language learners, especially ESL students, are also dealing with cultural expectations that can be quite different from what they are used to, and the emotions surrounding conflicting expectations can derail the learning process.

I recall feeling inadequate or stupid because the simplest interaction suddenly became difficult—going to the grocery store, getting a haircut, taking the bus—when my language was so minimal. It was hard to have any kind of self-confidence when I felt I was unable to be fully understood. I felt nervous to try out my new language for fear that I would mispronounce a word or that the interaction would be awkward.

When I returned from Moldova, I began teaching a section of ELD (English Language Development) Content, a class for ESL students. In working with these students, I am more aware now of the different modes students employ in the language acquisition process. There are those students who are fearless in their use of the language. They try things out and rush forward with their interactions with others, practicing the language constantly, trying out new words or phrases and not worrying whether they are saying things incorrectly. My Peace Corps colleague Colleen was this type of learner—she was more interested in making the attempt to talk and rarely worried that she didn't have the right word. She would keep trying until someone understood what she was trying to say. And then there are the students who try to get it right before they try things out in public, who want to have the sentence constructed in their heads before it gets said out loud. This was me in Moldova, and this was the source of much of my frustration. I was too afraid of sounding dumb, so I stopped myself from speaking until I was sure I had my sentences constructed correctly. But this meant that many things went unsaid. In my role as a teacher, I want to provide students the safety to be more like Colleen, to be fearless and free in their use of new language, and I want to be the teacher that Nadia was for me, giving students the space to clear their minds and express themselves with confidence.

The way we use language is so connected to our sense of identity, to who we are as people. When we are unable to communicate clearly, we can feel unseen, unknown, invisible. In Moldova, my self-confidence was shaken by my inability to connect with the people around me. Although I felt like a confident adult when I was speaking English, when I was surrounded by the Romanian language, I became an insecure child again. We all want to be understood. And when misunderstanding begins to be woven into the fabric of daily life, our sense of self can be shaken.

My breakdown in Nadia's apartment helped me to understand in a visceral way what so many English language learners experience on a daily basis in their classrooms. My new role as a language student gave me empathy for what many of my students feel when they aren't understood and don't understand. And it isn't just English language learners who struggle with the confidence surrounding language acquisition. When we ask native speakers to navigate academic language, it can also bring up a crisis in confidence.

My deeper understanding of this concept has changed the way I deal with students. The biggest change has come at the personal level of how I relate to my students. I try to build a strong foundation of compassion and patience with my ELD students and provide them a safe and supportive space to practice their new language skills. I try to pay close attention to their emotional well-being while also challenging them to work diligently at improving their language skills and providing them with a rigorous curriculum. I better recognize the fact that ESL students are not only trying to navigate a school system that includes six different teachers with six different learning styles each day, but they are also trying to do this while learning an entirely new culture and language. There is so much I don't know about what trauma students might have experienced before arriving in our classroom or how that trauma might be wrapped up in issues of language and identity.

In my ELD class, I try to give students chances to experiment and play with language in the no-holds-barred way that Colleen did in Moldova. We play theater games that I have adapted from my drama classes in order to bring a sense of play into the classroom. Playing charades with our vocabulary words can encourage even the most reluctant speaker to shout out the correct answer. One fall morning, students in my ELD reading class worked in pairs to create different types of vehicles, and when Edyn splayed out on the floor and Cesar stood next to him and acted out sailing down the street on a skateboard, everyone in the class knew the word, and laughed at the creative energy and spirit.

I also try to include multiple activities that allow the students to access language tied to their identities. One of the most successful projects was a performance piece based on Ping Chong's *Undesirable Elements* series (2013). In Ping Chong's original pieces, community members perform a choral documentary theater piece and tell their own stories within their own communities. In our version, students answered questions about their lives in written form first, and then their own written words were combined to create a performance piece for a small audience. Students were able to describe themselves and their immigration stories in words that they chose, in a safe and supportive space. When I first worked on this assignment in the spring of 2019, I had 31 students from eight different countries. Students shared stories about the origins of their names ("My name means my eyes and heart are like the ocean, beautiful and clean."), about their journeys to the United States ("I traveled by car, truck, bus, and plane. I came alone."), about their hopes and dreams for the future ("I hope my English will be better. I want to be a writer," "I want to start a good business. I can do it! Don't worry, self!"), about what the word "home" meant to them. At the end of the performance, they shared one piece of advice they would give to a new student who had just arrived in the United States. Their advice included: "If you want a good future, you need to follow the school rules," "Do ALL the homework," "You need to have good influences," and "You will have a life easier than you presently have." Yuna summed it up at the end, "Everything will be fine! Don't worry!" Students who took part in this performance used their own experiences to create a written and spoken piece that built their language proficiency while honoring their own individual stories.

The issues of language and identity go beyond the ESL classroom. In my drama classes, I weave in various opportunities for students to tell their own stories in their own voices before they attempt to take on new characters. And in my English classes, students write a family memoir based on an interview with an older family member. Their finished product is written in the voice of the person they interviewed, honoring that family member's story and voice. These activities offer students a chance to hear and value their own voices in an academic setting, and gain confidence with their own language use as they begin to step into new types of language.

My students often remind me how important it is to remember what Moldova taught me. One day in early October, I sat down next to "Angel," a student in my ELD Content class, to check in about the assignment we were working on. Angel had entered our school district in September of 2020 and had spent his first year of American high school in remote learning. The transition back to in-person learning seemed to be going mostly smoothly, and Angel was an active participant in class, raising his hand often to share his ideas. He seemed to be fairly comfortable speaking English, but writing things down was more of a struggle, as were new assignments that had directions different from what we had done before. The day's assignment involved creating a slideshow about hunter-gatherer life using some of the vocabulary words we had been studying for the past few weeks. As I looked over Angel's work, it was clear he hadn't understood the directions. I went through the first few slides and tried to explain to him what he was doing wrong and asked if he understood. Angel would nod and say, "Yes," and then make a change to the slide that showed he hadn't understood anything I was saying. After a few minutes of this I looked at Angel's face and saw that he was on the brink of tears. My mind flew across the miles and the years to that tiny Moldovan apartment, and I quickly realized that what Angel needed at this precise moment wasn't a critique of what he was doing wrong. He needed a moment to breathe, and he needed to be understood. I needed to attend to Angel as a human being, not just as a student to be taught. I paused, and I could see the frustration etched all over his face. So I pulled my phone out of my pocket, and used Google Translate to ask Angel if he was ok. I explained to him that I could see he was frustrated, and we could take a break if he wanted. Angel nodded and a few minutes later, I came back to him and this time, we slowly went through everything, and I broke things down into smaller pieces, and Angel got it. He found the thread of understanding, and he stitched together the assignment.

My breakdown in Nadia's apartment became my breakthrough moment in understanding the emotional minefield that language learning can be, whether it is learning a second (or third or fourth) language or learning how to navigate academic language. My classroom is still an academically rigorous one, but I approach the language process with more empathy, compassion, and patience. And a box of tissues.

CONCLUSION

One thing I would like the reader to take away from this piece is a deeper understanding of the emotional toll of language learning. Many teachers understand this on an intellectual level, but we can forget this in our own desires to get the information across as we try to "teach hard." I hope this essay is a reminder to look for the moments when we need to stop the lesson and pay attention, instead, to the learner. We need to look for more opportunities to help students be fearless in their language use by creating a safe space that clearly recognizes the connection between language and identity.

I also encourage teachers to notice what happens within themselves when learning something new, whether that new thing is a language, a new athletic or musical pursuit, or a new computer program mandated by a school district. Where do our emotions take us? Are we trying to get everything just right before we move on to the next lesson? Or are we willing to play a little and make mistakes along the way? How, as teachers, can we bring our own learning experiences into the classroom in an effort to better understand and help our students? It is always humbling when a teacher becomes a student again, and it's a reminder to address the emotions that arise along the way, especially when teaching something as intimately tied to identity as language.

RECOMMENDED READING

Kelin, D. A. (2009). *In Their Own Words: Drama with Young English Language Learners.* New Plays Incorporated.

This school year I have been teaching a drama class specifically for ESL students, and that has been an amazing chance to put much of my breakthrough into action. Daniel Kelin's (2009) book has been an invaluable resource for me.

Lahiri, J. (2015, December 7). Teach yourself Italian. *The New Yorker.*

Jhumpa Lahiri (2015) wrote an extraordinary piece about learning Italian that clearly captures the emotional aspects of language learning.

Swain, M. (2013). The inseparability of cognition and emotion in second language learning. *Language Teaching, 46*(2), 195–207.

For further reading on the emotional aspects of language learning, see Merrill Swain's article.

About Chapter 8

For **Kelly Crosby**, it was "too many late nights commenting" [on student papers] that brought growing discomfort with her ESL training and its focus on student error. Shaking off the "deficit thinking that is all around me and my students," Crosby chooses the road less taken to focus on what her University of California, Davis students have to say rather than the number of errors they make.

Crosby experiments with her written responses to her students' drafts, first by sitting back and simply being an appreciative reader. Her discoveries about how and when to comment will no doubt reassure those of us who've also struggled with how to respond. Crosby notes: "Teaching writing to English learners offers the chance to do so much with [their writing]. . . . Not everything matters all the time. Language develops with practice and encouragement. Errors happen to all of us. Feedback is meant to keep a writer writing."

CHAPTER 8

Changing Perspectives on Written Feedback

Kelly Crosby

I am a writing teacher, and my students are writers.

Interrogating and revising how I give written comments on student writing as a second language writing teacher at the University of California, Davis, has not been revolutionary nor groundbreaking. Instead, it has been messy and problematic. Entertaining questions about why I teach, how I teach, and what I teach, has changed me as a teacher, even in my 25th year.

I'm a full-time lecturer, with a master's degree in TESOL, teaching in a writing program. In the last couple of years, I have spent time taking inventory of what I have—decades of valuable teaching experience and a degree from a prestigious program, and what I don't have—a degree in composition. I have been in my current position for 10 years, mostly teaching first-year English learners in sheltered courses that support their English language development while working toward the fulfillment of a writing requirement. When I was hired, the university was experiencing a massive enrollment surge in EL students. My training and experience felt important and valuable.

In cross-campus conversations I noticed that many non–second language writing teachers questioned why English learner students were even admitted when they couldn't communicate in class: "I feel awful putting [international/multilingual students] in groups for peer review workshops when it's so hard to even understand them," they complained. Another commented that she "failed students for their own good so that they'd learn now what they need to do with their writing in English instead of getting fired from a job for how bad it is." With this mindset, the expectations around language seemed to outweigh the development of students as writers. I took this messaging as a call to action. At the time I didn't see or acknowledge the colonial, racist undertones in this negative perspective. However, I realize that I silently endorsed the concern and bias by making my course and its expectations overwhelming, maintaining my status as both the authority and the support.

My own rubrics and written feedback had a laser-like focus on everything. I often assessed progress and success in terms of effective editing and organization. One of my rubrics for an assignment from the spring of 2016 has 23 items I was evaluating. To put myself as the authority of everything in writing was an impossible task. I was constantly thinking about what

I would do, how I would teach a grammar point, and how I would have enough time to comment on drafts as they came in.

Still operating with unreasonable expectations, near the end of spring quarter 2017, I spent three consecutive late nights giving feedback on drafts of long student papers for two sections of a first-year writing course for multilingual students. As the hours passed, I wasn't enjoying myself; I rarely reacted—internally or on paper—to students' ideas and questioned whether I was a good writing teacher at all, given what I was reading. Looking back at a student's draft from that time, I saw I had included directives like, "Break for a new paragraph here," or "Be sure to include your name, the date, the course, and the word count in your final draft." My written comments were also corrective and abundant, ranging from highlighting grammar, spelling, and punctuation errors, to APA in-text citation adjustments, to comments about my confusion while reading. By the time I'd returned all drafts back to students with comments, I was depleted.

I got the final drafts back about a week later and found myself writing new comments like, "I don't see evidence of revision here," or, "I see more clarity in your writing through editing of grammar errors, but I'm still distracted by the organization." I remember opening earlier drafts and looking at my comments, then going to the final draft and zooming in on the spaces where I was almost *willing* change to happen. Students changed a few words, parts of speech, or moved a few sentences or paragraphs, but didn't fully seize control of their papers. Disheartened, I then had to compile final grades. I examined my rubric—the one I had used for several quarters with this course—and was uncomfortable with its breadth and the way it pulled down grades for editing issues. What mattered most? How was I to evaluate their writing when I was most concerned with compliance with my suggestions?

Ultimately my practices were unsustainable, and I needed to find new ways to use instructional time as well as my own time responding to writing. My approaches were taking the joy out of writing, likely for me and for my students. Throughout my career I've consistently asked students to reflect on their writing, typically in cover memos with essays or major assignments. At the time of this breakthrough, I was using portfolio assessment, so students wrote an end-of-term two-page reflective piece that captured their development as writers and changes they'd noticed in their writing skills. Seeking insight and motivation to make a change I read this set of portfolio reflections carefully. I noticed several students consistently equate good writing with grammatical accuracy. For example, students lamented *still* having grammar errors in their writing, naming accuracy as a primary goal in the future. One student even said that because of grammar errors and challenges paraphrasing, they had a "long way to go in order to become a true writer." The way I had perceived my role as a second language writing specialist, always addressing language and writing, felt limited and limiting, leaving me doubling down on doubts about whether writing development could flourish in sheltered courses like mine. Perhaps with a new perspective from outside of my own training in linguistics I could shift my focus and foster the writing identities my students wanted.

SEEKING A NEW PERSPECTIVE

Our educational systems recognize that students have unique needs and assets, yet the separate way English language learners have historically been taught is problematic, controversial, and divisive. If the goal is about language as separate from ideas, thoughts, and arguments, we are left without a reason to communicate. I've seen criticism of a focus on standard English in scholarship across disciplines. Mina Shaughnessy (1977), advocate for students of basic writing, described the obsession that traditional writing instructors had with error and the fuel of remediation that kept it alive in *Errors and Expectations: A Guide for the Teacher of Basic Writing*. This fixation on identifying and fixing errors is also the basis for so much of the TESOL scholarship, almost as if our place as experts is cemented by identifying what student writers are doing wrong. Fortunately, current scholarship calls on us to do better, offering more equitable approaches such as critical language awareness (Britton & Leonard, 2020) and linguistically responsive pedagogy (Tomaš and Shapiro, 2021).

Arizona State University professor of rhetoric and composition Asao Inoue (2015) casts an even darker shadow on the implications of weaponizing language and "error." He writes, "We live in a racist society, one that recreates well-known, well-understood, racial hierarchies in populations based on things like judgments of student writing that use a local Standardized Edited American English (SEAE) with populations of people who do not use that discourse daily—judging apples by the standards of oranges. Racism has always been a part of writing assessment at all levels" (p. 6).

I was learning and was deeply uncomfortable. My teacher energy felt confused. Though I felt I had been offering students what they needed and wanted—concrete knowledge of when and how their words and sentences were understood by me, my feedback practices lacked balance. Understanding a writer is far deeper than words, but for my English learner students, clear sentences were concrete evidence of good writing. Most had studied writing for high-stakes timed tests linked to high school graduation and college admissions. They looked to me for signaling and repair guidance, even when I believed most errors were insignificant. Contemplating the implications of my corrective written comments, I became concerned that I'd been judging student writing against the unrealistic target Inoue described.

I also began thinking more deeply about my students, the pressures they faced to write across courses, genres, and disciplines. Former Cornell writing center tutor Faiza Ahmad (2019) wrote an open letter in response to an act of discrimination against Chinese students at Duke. Raising empathy for the incredible efforts of multilingual and international students, she described an interaction with a tutee:

> I told her that it was quite an incredible feat to learn a language with not even so much as a remotely similar script as your mother tongue and within a couple of years manage to write an eight-page paper on philosophy, of all things. In response to my incredulation, she shrugged her shoulders and said "I guess I don't have a choice." (para. 12)

Ever since I discovered Ahmad's open letter, I've shared it with my classes. Learning from experts and scholars is valuable and productive, but hearing directly from my students grounds me as a teacher.

ADOPTING A NEW PRACTICE

"Reimagining practice means recognizing that teachers must reflect on what lies behind their teaching decisions, the assignments they design, and the comments they make about student work" (Zoch et al., 2016). Every decision matters. It was time to move beyond discomfort and self-criticism into new ideas and revised practices. I felt like a student again, reading articles and having conversations about new topics in familiar territory. I read TESOL publications and asked for recommendations outside of language scholarship, too. I wanted to know where other teachers stood on the question of attention to language and error. We all teach multilingual students, so how do we feel collectively about what to say in written comments? When I asked compositionist colleagues how they addressed error in student writing, they often said it wasn't a priority for them and they usually overlooked it. Fellow second language writing colleagues, most with a stronger education in linguistics than in composition studies, were more likely to notice and address error, especially when it was patterned and persistent.

For the next couple of quarters, before making substantial changes to assignments, I made a conscious effort to pull back on my comments, in number and in breadth, on all assignments.

Resisting marginal comments was hard for me; I kept going back to a time early in my career when a former supervisor told me she always commented on everything, thinking students wouldn't learn without it. Instead, I took measures to center myself in my work as a *writing teacher* because I was teaching *writers* who spoke other languages, had learned about writing in other places, and had the ability to interact with the world around them—to shape it and be shaped by it.

Given my previous impulse to comment on everything, to drive a student's revision and editing in a whirlwind of correction, I first had to back off, put down my pen or fingers at my keyboard, and just read their drafts.

In doing this, I had no motivation other than reading for purpose and response to the assignment prompt. Adjusting my commenting patterns away from grammar and mechanical errors reduced my overall comments significantly and actually had me reading student writing very differently. I was now reading for what was present, what the student was saying and doing, instead of what was missing or in error. Following the advice of Nancy Sommers (2013), I looked for strengths that allowed me to eventually respond to them as a teacher, not an editor. Ideas, not solutions. Matsuda and Cox (2011) showed that reading a student's writing from beginning to end gives the reader a sense of the student's organization of ideas "on its own terms" (p. 11). Orienting myself away from my responsibility to compare their language or structure against a standard English created space for my students and their writing. I wasn't reading with correction or my own authority in mind anymore, but instead to join them in their thoughts and developing ideas, and I imagine that the burden was lifting for them and for me, as I was no longer the "stranger who reads it with a lawyer's eyes, searching for flaws" that Shaughnessy (1977, p. 391) described.

However, this is not to say that I ignored students' need for grammar-related feedback. I came back to the middle ground and began to synthesize my practice, to give comments related to purpose. For example, where I would once make a note on an incorrect verb tense, I would now read the complete idea and notice *as their reader* whether I had lost track of time in the context of their sentence and paragraph. If I felt lost, I would let them know—maybe I noticed signals about the past, but the verb put me in the future—and that interrupted my focus. I also began and continue to engage directly with student idea development. I have students include memos to me with questions to answer in my comments. They direct me to where to give feedback, so the student retains agency. For example, in an assignment where students are analyzing Ahmad's techniques of argument in her open letter, I responded to a student's question about one of the techniques: "The third technique you mention is your best sample, and I would like you to add how (in addition to having a quote from a member of the intended audience) it strengthens the actual claim—focus on the actual content of the quote and the claim." I communicate with my students as decision-making writers and can offer more meaningful revision suggestions, praise, and direction.

Prioritizing my reactions and responses to their writing actually made teaching writing a more emotional experience. Focusing on words, accuracy, sentence structure, and form, while concrete, is usually unemotional. In hindsight, I see that my comments were scattershot, and I had created assignments and rubrics that necessitated noticing everything. I perpetuated the myth of perfection in writing, working against what I actually believed in. I've learned how impactful written comments can be. They convey what really matters, what the reader has paused to notice. I'd missed the forest for the trees with my students. I'm glad I gave myself the chance to try again and to revise my commenting practices to be a better reader and listener.

CONCLUSION

Like I said earlier, this is by no means revolutionary, but it is transformative to me. Perhaps some of the essence of my conundrum comes from my own education and years as a student seeing writing as a product to be assessed. Perhaps it also comes from the (not so) quiet legacy of colonialism in foreign and second language instruction, mixed with the complicated nature of English being both the medium of instruction and the assessed content of a course. Or more important, my professional evolution has been in the spirit of joining—me with my students as writers who need to revise and get feedback in order to keep on going, and my language-centric field of TESOL with process and idea-driven principles of composition. Like writing, teaching is a social action. I needed to hear from others about how they teach. I also had to make space for gradual change and experimentation.

I love that I've evolved as a writing teacher by changing the way I give written comments to students. The one-on-one interactions with writers and writing have softened me and have given me a renewed but different sense of purpose. Where I once took on the weight of language and accuracy, I now afford myself the time to interact more with ideas and development. I want my comments to students to anchor them in something they know, an idea they have, or even a new concept from class. They are intended to serve a bridge to in-class instruction, keeping us all connected to the teaching and learning that happens every week.

Teaching writing to English learners offers the chance to do so much with text, a more complicated continuum than I'd realized. Not everything matters all the time. Language develops with practice and encouragement. Errors happen to all of us. Feedback is meant to keep a writer writing. We can all be writers, regardless of the language(s) we speak and write.

RECOMMENDED READING

Conference on College Composition and Communication. (2020, May). CCCC statement on second language writing and multilingual writers. https://cccc.ncte.org /cccc/resources/positions/secondlangwriting

Matsuda, P. K. (2012). Let's face it: Language issues and the writing program administrator. *WPA: Writing Program Administration, 36*(1), 141–163.

Matsuda's article and the CCCC statement offer compassion and dignity to multilingual student writers and those of us teaching them.

Motha, S. (2014). *Race, empire, and English language teaching.* Teachers College Press.

Motha's book educates English Language teachers about the power-hungry, imperialistic roots of the field then encourages us to evolve.

About Chapter 9

Veteran high school teacher **Rob Rogers** finds his personal life on display when he is forced to teach from home during the pandemic. While he feels great discomfort with a camera recording the antics of his children as he tries to teach remotely, he also recognizes that "we [he and his students] were, all of us, on the same team, trying to outmaneuver this thing that had separated us from each other. . . ." In the end, almost nothing is the same as it used to be and perhaps for the better.

Rogers reexamines the role of personal connection and emotional engagement in learning, especially as these are being challenged by distance and isolation. He discovers the costs of opening up his world to students, but also the freedom it brings.

CHAPTER 9

Personal and Confidential

What the Pandemic Taught Me About My Relationship With Students

Rob Rogers

I don't remember when it was that my mentor said it, or what had brought me to his classroom door that day. I was a first-year teacher, so it might have been my frustration with unruly, unresponsive students; or the teacher next door who stormed into my classroom on a daily basis to tell me to keep those unruly, unresponsive students in order; or even the parents of students who called to ask, complain about, or try to negotiate their children's grades. He was someone who had managed to remain his smart, subtle, witty self in a profession I felt sure had already broken me down.

"You can't take anything personally," he told me. "These kids don't know you. Their parents don't know you. If they did, you'd probably get along great. You, on the other hand, get to see and deal with everything going on in their lives, things that have nothing to do with you or your class. So don't make it about you."

His advice got me through the next 15 years of teaching, allowed me to stay passionate about my students and my subjects while cultivating a kind of detachment from everything else. I felt I had to separate who I was as a teacher from who I was as a person for the same reason I told my creative writing students not to see criticism of their stories as referendums on themselves. "You are not your work," I insisted to them and to myself, and I believed it. Students might love me or hate me; parents might praise me or complain about me, but none of them could really judge me because they had no way of seeing or knowing about my life outside of the classroom.

Until they did.

I've heard some of my fellow teachers talk about how the COVID-19 pandemic brought them back to their first year of teaching. For me, it wasn't just the overwhelming amount of work, the need to master new technologies overnight, or the necessity of coming up with everything, from curriculum to coping strategies, from scratch. It was the realization of the nightmare I used to have every summer, the one where I was standing in front of my classroom completely unprepared and utterly exposed. Having to teach online, at home, not only stripped away my privacy but made it all but impossible to remain detached. Just like that, my children were no longer adorable little faces in a photograph at the edge of my desk. They were very real, very active little people who climbed onto my shoulders while I tried to teach, who shouted out answers to the questions I posed to students, and who struggled, noisily, with their own online classrooms just a few feet away. I'd gone years without revealing even my first name to my students. Now they'd been given a backstage pass to the messiest parts of my personal life.

And I had been given one into theirs. The things students or their counselors used to confide to me—stories of angry parents, dying relatives, homes that were broken or confusing or just messy and loud—all of these came through in high definition during our online classes, at least until my students became savvy enough to disguise them. The problems I'd viewed in pre-pandemic days as being distractions from whatever we were doing in the classroom became, simply, the reality of my students' lives, magnified by the crisis we were living through together. I still wanted to make sure my students understood Thoreau's idea of living deliberately and what *The Great Gatsby* had to say about pursuing the American Dream in a world of fundamental inequality. Now, though, I also wanted to know how my students were coping with isolation; how one, in particular, was managing being cared for by his slightly older sister while his parents attended a funeral in Mexico; how another was feeling the pressure to play football with a broken foot because that weekend might be the only time, in a COVID-shortened year, that scouts from the schools where he wants to apply would ever see him.

I felt vulnerable, exposed, worried that my laptop's camera would reveal to the world in general and my students in particular everything about myself I'd tried for so long to conceal. But there was another feeling, too, that came with exposure: the feeling that we were, all of us, on the same team, trying to outmaneuver this thing that had separated us from each other and caused us to wonder whether anything like what we'd thought about as normal would ever come around again. It helped that I'd been freed by the virus from my traditional role as enforcer of classroom rules. I didn't have to worry about smuggled snacks. I could mute any student who was being disruptive. And the only dress code violation I had to contend with was the one student who forgot to put on a shirt before class.

In those moments I was able to imagine a classroom in which we all cared about and related to each other as human beings, a place where the process of learning felt more fulfilling because it was a shared journey and not a forced march. I imagined entering a physical room the way I came into our virtual meetings, asking the young man in front of me about the LEGO build on the shelf behind him or the cat who crawled into his arms while we spoke. When I met with students one-on-one during online "office hours" to help them with their essays, I felt we shared a kind of casual intimacy, a meeting of the minds that was personal to a degree I had never experienced in the classroom.

That dream of a shared experience began to fracture the moment our school transitioned from the "distance learning" of the early pandemic days to a hybrid model in which some students returned to the classroom while others remained at home. Having to split my attention between two very different groups made it more difficult for me to check in with students, even as their behavior made me want to. Was the student at the back of the class constantly looking at his phone because a family member was sick? Was he waiting for the results of his own COVID test? Or was he just checking in with his friends—and if he was, was that necessarily a bad thing? What about the young woman on Zoom who disappeared from my screen five minutes after class began, claiming each day that her microphone or her camera or her wireless connection no longer worked? Was she feeling isolated? Depressed? Left behind? Or was she merely lazy?

I asked the same questions of myself. The pandemic had eaten away the enamel of my detachment, leaving me a bundle of raw nerves. I felt irritable, frustrated, and exposed, unable to recognize my students behind their masks but convinced they could see right through the layers of my personal protective equipment to the fear and anxiety I tried so hard to keep hidden. At first, worried about the virus, I wondered whether I should have returned to the classroom at all. As the year ground toward its conclusion, I wondered whether I should leave for good.

It was at that point that I remembered what I always told those students who were nervous about classroom presentations. "Trust me," I told them, "No one in the audience is thinking about you. They're thinking about what's for lunch, or about practice this afternoon, or something someone posted on Instagram. If you can get them to think about what you're saying for a few seconds, you're lucky." I'd been so worried about what my students saw when they looked at me that I'd forgotten to see them. It wasn't until I was required, on the first day of the new school year, to read the results of a survey my school had conducted on the effects of the COVID-19 pandemic that I caught a glimpse of the last year through their eyes.

"I find myself very stressed and constantly thinking about how everything is; however, I'm mostly still trying my best," one student wrote. "I don't let it get to me emotionally, but I think people should understand that for a lot of students . . . the pandemic has brought about an academic nightmare." The reality of that "nightmare" was something almost all of the respondents could agree upon, though they were divided as to its causes. While one pleaded for all students to return to campus, "I don't understand how people in Sacramento and in Southern California can be in school five days a week but we cannot . . . I know how much better it will be if we are able to go back," another argued for staying at home, "I think they can be a little bit less forcing for kids to come back on campus." The distracted behavior I thought I'd witnessed looked very different from the other side of the screen: "Online learning is much harder than being in person. It is a pain to have to try and get teachers to believe in our integrity!"

I had thought that having unexpected, unprecedented (and in most cases, unwanted) access to each other's private lives over the last year and a half would provide my students and myself with new levels of understanding. I had forgotten what 20 years' worth of reality television should have taught me: that a camera, however intrusive, can only show what is on the surface, that true understanding requires a deeper form of communication. I'd always tried to build a classroom where every student could feel at home: making allowance for different learning styles and preferences, finding ways for students to connect what we were discussing to ideas and experiences they already understood. What my students were asking for now seemed like something different: "Be more understanding to the students, especially those who are . . . at home the majority of the time. Although we do understand that teachers have it just as difficult as we do, there needs to be a mutual balance and acknowledgement due to these unprecedented challenges. A mentality that is more compassionate, more forgiving."

Several months later, and with no end to the pandemic in sight, I'm struggling to do just that by finding ways to let my students' lived experience become a part of their classroom experience. It's easiest in my creative writing classroom where so many of my students have chosen to write about their journey through COVID-19 as part of an autobiographical writing assignment. I'm able to let them tell their stories—but also to remind them that to truly be theirs, their stories have to focus not on what happened *to* them, but on how their own actions and decisions shaped the course of their lives. It's harder in my junior English classes, where the curriculum offers fewer opportunities for self-expression. Last week, I began a class by asking each student to post a photograph he or she had taken during the first year of the pandemic. Some of the students showed themselves on camping or fishing trips with their parents; others had pictures of friends they missed or of a blank computer screen, or of beds they say they hardly ever left. It was a reminder to everyone in the room how the one truly unifying thing about this experience is how different it has been for all of us.

I don't want to forget what my mentor shared with me during my first year of teaching. Yet the words I have become determined to live by are those of Tony Hoagland, one of my favorite poets, who in his poem "Personal" wrote about how much more painful and difficult life can be when one takes things personally—but also fuller, richer, and more complete:

Get over it, they said
at the School of Broken Hearts

but I couldn't and I didn't and I don't
believe in the clean break;

I believe in the compound fracture
served with a sauce of dirty regret,

I believe in saying it all
and taking it all back

and saying it again for good measure
while the air fills up with *I'm-Sorries*

like wheeling birds
and the trees look seasick in the wind.

In a world where all of us seem to be seeing and learning so much more about each other than we might like, encouraging students to bring their life experiences to the classroom in a manner that is meaningful to them gives those students something the pandemic has taken away from them in so many ways: control over their own lives. I'm still trying not to take things personally. But taking people personally is helping me become the kind of teacher my students need, and the kind I have always wanted to be.

CONCLUSION

I wish I could say that my life in the classroom has become easier in the months since I wrote those words. If anything, it's become more difficult. My students have seemed less engaged, more distracted, and less respectful than at any point in my teaching career. At times, I have found myself growing frustrated and confused. Weren't these the same students who were desperate to be back on campus after the lockdown? Why were they playing video games instead of taking notes? Why didn't they want to learn?

I thought I might find the answers at a seminar, "Teaching Struggling Brains: Improving Mental Health, Focus, Motivation and Learning in a Distressed, Digital Generation," held across the continent in Boston. On the morning I was supposed to leave, however, a family emergency caused me to miss my flight, and I had to attend the conference on Zoom. The information came through loud and clear—if anything, it was easier to take notes on my laptop at home than it would have been in a conference hall. But I was disappointed that I wouldn't be able to talk to, have lunch with, or swap ideas with any of the other teachers in attendance, especially since I already felt so isolated on my own campus.

That experience helped me understand what my students had been going through and were still going through. As one of the conference speakers, *Learning to Change* author Dr. Andy Hargreaves (2022), said, "During the pandemic, cognitive engagement was not too hard, and sometimes it was even better. What was harder was emotional engagement." Like me, my students, through no fault of their own, had been placed in a situation where they couldn't talk or share or commiserate with friends or potential friends at a time when they most needed those connections. My students did want to learn—but that wasn't the main reason they wanted to come to school, or the primary concern they had while they were there.

I am now learning ways to better acknowledge the lives and concerns my students have outside of the classroom, and to help them transition to the kind of learning we need to do together. Those transitions can come in many forms, from taking time to ask students about their interests, to asking them to begin class by writing down the things that are on their minds. After all, I tell them, writing about a difficult experience you couldn't control can make your life start to feel like your own again. It's certainly helped me.

RECOMMENDED READING

Bonnello, C. (2019). *Underdogs*. Unbound Digital.

> Books like *The Hunger Games, Ready Player One,* and *Scythe* tell the stories of teenage protagonists struggling to save a ruined world from dangers for which the adults in their lives never prepared them. The series *Underdogs* takes this idea a step further: Its young, neurodiverse protagonists must work with each other to save the world from an apocalypse.

Dennis-Tiwary, T. (2022). *Future tense: Why anxiety is good for you (even though it feels bad)*. Piatkus.

> Rather than trying to "cure" anxious students (or, for that matter, anxious teachers) neuroscientist Dennis-Tiwary argues that we should view anxiety as a useful sign, a tool our bodies and minds use to communicate something important to us. Approaching anxiety and the ways it manifests itself in the classroom, from digital distraction to academic avoidance, with curiosity rather than frustration can help students understand why they're feeling the way they are, and what they can learn from it.

Gonzalez, J. (2021, May 16). No more easy button: A suggested approach to post-pandemic teaching. *Cult of Pedagogy*. https://www.cultofpedagogy.com/easy-button/

> Rather than rushing to get back to the way things were before the pandemic, Gonzalez argues that teachers should learn from the ways online and hybrid education exposed some of the flaws of traditional teaching methods. In particular, she argues for more collaborative, hands-on projects, more feedback from teachers and peers (but fewer grades!) and a more inclusive classroom experience that allows for deeper relationships between students and teachers.

About Chapter 10

Community college teacher **James Wilson** hides their personal identity from their students, convinced that their "coming out" might "take up too much space and get in the way of the learning that has to happen." But hiding means they build "a new closet" around themself, one that keeps their students at a distance and limits the chances of creating mutual trust and growth.

Wilson's breakthrough—self acceptance and an active role in supporting LGBTQIA+ students across campus—does not happen in one fell swoop. It's a gradual realization, one filled with doubt and hesitation, but also resolve. In the end, Wilson feels responsible for helping all their students to be themselves without fear. "When I assume my own power and present myself as I am to my students, I can then invite my students to do the same."

CHAPTER 10

Becoming Somebody
Queering the Classroom and Resisting "Neutral"

James Andrew Wilson

2014. My nail polish is a subtle shade—nearly the color of my own flesh, but yes, there's a little sheen to catch the light. As I slide the book under the document camera and point to a line in the text, I hear two students giggle in the back. Immediately, I am certain that my shiny fingernails, subtle as they are, are the subject of the laughter. Or perhaps it's my insecurity, which is right under the surface today. When I came into school today with this nail polish, I feared the stares of the young men in my class, the ones who, through no fault of their own, remind me of my tormentors in middle school. But it's not they who are laughing; it's a pair of young women. I lose my train of thought, stumble, feel my cheeks going red. I recompose myself and return to the text.

I come to teaching English through performance. After a BA in English and drama and then professional theater training, I got into playwriting, and via a master's degree in creative writing, I backed my way into English teaching at the community college level. When I began teaching writing, I thought often of my theater training. Jacques Lecoq, the theater guru of sorts who founded the school I attended, is famous for saying about his teaching, "I am nobody. I am only a neutral point through which you must pass in order to better articulate your own theatrical voice. I am only there to place obstacles in your path, so you can find your own way round them" (as quoted in Esslin, 1999). When I began teaching while in grad school, this was a beautiful idea to me—that the teacher is a conduit who redirects you, who makes your life difficult for a while in such a way that you grow. And in order to do this, they themselves don't really have any notable identity as such.

While Lecoq and his pedagogy are French to the core, this idea of the teacher as a "nobody" meshes pretty well with the very American idea of teachers as selfless and self-sacrificial. We'll work 13-hour days and buy our own school supplies because it's worth it to make a difference in students' lives. It's all worth it for the joy it gives us to serve. It's not about us.

Teaching is, of course, a service-oriented profession. You don't get into this profession unless you can tolerate some sacrifice and self-effacement. You hold your students' hands just as long as you need to, until the moment you can let go. You then fade into the background while they walk on alone, living the rest of their lives having—we hope!—taken something from our time together. Our purpose is the students' growth, and so we really don't matter beyond what we do to shape students' journeys. So yes, as Lecoq says, we, as teachers, are "nobody."

On the other hand, the value Lecoq places on neutrality reflects a familiar ideology that any teacher with an identity that is not "neutral," a teacher who's a "somebody," may take up too much space and get in the way of the learning that has to happen. I know of a teacher who, arguably by this same logic, lost her job as a teacher after students saw her tattoos on a hot day. Even where I teach, in my safe home state of California, I fear that a teacher who calls too much attention to themselves will be seen as putting on a show for their own narcissistic satisfaction, not for their students' growth. I may be a performer by training, I tell myself, but now I'm a teacher. It's not a performance. Dial it down.

It is of course, not lost on me that the idea that a teacher is just a "neutral point" has a Eurocentric, White supremacist lens built into it. I was aware, even at the start of my career 10 years ago, that only certain bodies—white, male—have access to the kind of "neutrality" that Lecoq talks about here. Even in a profession that is overwhelmingly female, I have seen how students treat my female colleagues with less respect than my male colleagues, who seem to carry more authority by default. In a misogynistic society, male is still seen as neutral, and therefore more powerful, to many students. And yet, here I am, a white male, and I can't shake the idea that I should disappear at the front of the classroom.

Plus as it happens, a quest to attain some kind of teacherly "neutrality" chimes well with an innate desire I have, in spite of my theatrical tendencies, to blend in, to not take up too much space in anyone's field of vision.

And so in those first quarters as an adjunct, I make a point to present myself as a professional—boring—version of myself. And I seek a kind of stability too: I develop a pet theory that the tone you set at the start of the semester is more or less the tone you should keep throughout. A teacher should be somewhat constant, predictable—neutral.

It doesn't take me long to discover that in embracing this philosophy of neutral professionalism I have created a new closet for myself. Outside of work, this is a time of discovering new personal outlets for my own queerness, which seems to be in rapid evolution. And yet on campus I stay buttoned up, "neutral." Straight. I'm not out to anyone at work, and while I don't truly fear being discriminated against on my progressive campus, I think that as a new adjunct I'd best keep my head down, get good evaluations, avoid standing out.

One Sunday night before Monday class, I am in my bathroom at home rubbing off the nail polish I put on before going out on Friday night. I feel a familiar shame. The shame is about the nail polish *remover*, not the polish itself. It's about my cowardice. Who am I hiding from? My students? The boys in the back of the class? My colleagues? Does anyone care? Really, what is the worst that could happen? In anger and embarrassment, I decide that I will never again remove nail polish for work.

2017, August. I've just begun a full-time position as an English instructor at a community college I haven't worked at before. Prior to the first day, we are asked to indicate our "teaching interests" to be put on a slide that will be shown to faculty and staff on All College Day, the Friday before the semester begins. I make a point to put "queer literature" on my list. I want to be out here. Right away. No more hiding.

When my slide comes up, I'm supposed to stand up in the front row. I feel the weight of the stares of a full auditorium on my back. When the Vice President of Instruction reads out "queer literature," I don't think my ears deceive me when I hear an audible reaction from the crowd: an intake of breath that suggests recognition, delight. I have never felt more visible at work. As I'm leaving the auditorium, a colleague from the social justice program approaches. Perhaps I'd like to work with them? When I return to my office, I find an email from another colleague, a social science instructor near retirement who'd like to know if I want to take over advising for the Queer Straight Alliance (QSA) club. It's all happening so quickly.

Before starting my full-time position, I do several rounds of job hunting. At first I have no luck, but by the time I am writing applications the third time around, I have begun to understand my queer identity is a strength. From a pragmatic—not to say cynical—perspective, I see that it distinguishes me from other applicants. It gives search committees something to hold onto immediately, even if my complicated theater and English background is a little hard to understand.

It also feels better. I learn, the third time around, to quit trying to tell committees what I think they want to hear and to tell them who I am, show them what I have to say. And when I get an interview for the job I want most and the president asks me how I'd like to shape the college, I say, very sincerely, that I'd like to help make space for queer students to feel at home on this campus.

It works. I get the job.

I use this jump in professional status to let my definition of "professional" come out of the closet finally: nail polish—yes!—plus dangly earrings, louder shirts, an occasional subtle lip balm. And whatever I feared happening in my early adjunct days is not happening now. I am respected, courted even, by folks from around campus who want my contributions.

I recognize that the security of my position as a full-timer, even before tenure, allows me a freedom I just couldn't feel as an adjunct. I see concrete proof every day that my college wants me here, that it has invested in me and wants to make good on that investment. I was gay in the interview and here I am gay on campus— I made myself fully visible to the hiring committee and the college still chose me. This material stability erodes my cowardice a bit. In moments I doubt my choice to be so visible, I tell myself that I'm simply fulfilling a promise I made to be a queer advocate on this campus. My self-expression is not just for me, it's for the students. It serves a purpose.

2017, September. My new full-time position has allowed me to feel more confident in the classroom itself, and I am coming to see that bringing myself more openly to the classroom is not just good for me but actually has enormous pedagogical value. In my critical thinking class, my students watch a video on the AIDS Quilt at the start of a unit in which they will research and write about the tactics of an activist movement that interests them. HIV/AIDS has particular meaning for me on an academic and personal level. I bring in a copy of my PhD dissertation and show a chapter I wrote on the AIDS Quilt. I show them my bibliography and even share some of the sources I used: articles, an interactive app, the documentary. The goal is to personalize and humanize the research process. At a certain moment in the discussion it feels appropriate to tell them my uncle died of AIDS when I was a child; that if I have been able to live a relatively normal life as a gay person now, it is in no small part because of the AIDS activism of the '80s and '90s—like the AIDS Quilt—that demanded the attention of the American public, of the authorities; that I chose this topic in part because of the emotional connection I have to it. My voice cracks. I find myself getting a little emotional. The room goes quiet, and I feel the rapt attention of 25 or so students as I shift from "neutral" authority figure to emotionally vulnerable equal. It feels as if the stakes have been raised. This research assignment now seems to matter more than it could have had I not revealed myself to my students in this way. We move on to discuss choosing a topic.

In her book *Teaching Queer*, college composition professor Stacey Waite (2017) wonders what "queer" writing might look like, what a queer writing class might look like, what it is to be a queer teacher. She shares her experiments of trying to invent a praxis of composition built on the queer theory of Butler (1999), Warner (1991), Foucault (1980), and others. In some ways she is the anti-Lecoq; she is specifically *not* neutral. In fact, her conceit is that as a queer teacher she has something particular to bring to her students, a nonnormative outlook that might encourage nonnormative forms of thinking and writing for her students, whatever their gender or orientation.

As I read, I fill the margins with notes and questions. One important personal lesson for me here is that she is not apologizing for her queerness but rather framing it as the basis of her unique and important contribution to her students' development. How can I treat my own queerness in this way? How can I start believing that my students are in fact better off because they have a queer teacher like me? If I could believe that in my heart, I would be less worried about my fingernails, more integrated, happier.

But the point of Waite's book is not that teachers benefit from being out. The point is that students benefit from writing queerly. They learn to question received forms (the five-paragraph essay, the thesis statement, the well-structured paragraph) to create the forms of writing that their ideas demand. They liberate themselves from prescriptive writing rules and find a writing that reflects them and their ideas.

While I am inspired by this book, these ideas feel pretty abstract to me. What would a queer pedagogy really look like in a community college composition classroom? I don't have answers yet.

But I can begin by being more open with my students. I find that by default, the hierarchy from teacher to students enforces a distance between me standing at the board and the students sitting at their desks. I have also found that moments arise in the classroom when an opportunity presents itself to cross that distance. I have seen how using an example from my own life to illustrate a concept does something to the room. I mention my late uncle or my partner, I talk about my experience as a closeted college student, I acknowledge my own vulnerabilities in the classroom right now, I show emotion when it arises. Usually in these moments, a silence crystalizes in the room. I feel us, as a class, moving over a threshold toward some kind of shared trust.

That kind of vulnerability is a way of taking up space I wouldn't have felt comfortable with in my first quarters of teaching. But I now know that the space that I take for a few minutes in class is not just for me; it opens a door for students to bring parts of themselves they might have kept at home. It suggests that there is some safety here.

I no longer seek "neutrality" and I am most definitely not "nobody."

But I don't feel as if I'm done with this journey. Though the goalposts have moved in a queerer direction, I still find myself carefully monitoring the way I present myself at work. It's no longer about the nail polish. It's deeper now. I still feel fear, though the fear has become less precise. I'm not even really sure what I fear people seeing—nor what I think would happen if they did see it.

2017, September. At the first meeting of the QSA, the students begin, of course, with names and pronouns. As each person introduces themself— she/her, they/them, she/they, he or she, I don't give a fuck, hmm . . . today I'll go with him—I'm floored by their ability to embrace the messiness of gender, at least in this room. I sense on one hand a lightness: "'Whatever' is fine for me." On the other hand, everyone here takes this seriously. What I don't sense is shame.

Later, at home, as I'm recounting all this to my partner, I say, "I think if I were 19 right now, I would use 'they.'" When I was coming of age, I didn't have access to the language they do. I deeply admire their ease with the possibilities within themselves, and yet it feels foreign to me. When my partner asks me why I don't just use "they" anyway, I tell him it would be so conspicuous for someone my age to use that Gen Z language. The ship has sailed on that kind of self-discovery. And for a professor! It would almost be a little embarrassing.

Working so closely with the QSA is humbling. I don't feel like the authority here; on the contrary, it's I who am learning. Many of these students live with difficulties I never had to manage as a college student—unsupportive parents but no financial freedom, insane work schedules, long commutes, isolation, mental health challenges—and yet here they are affirming themselves without apology, affirming each other. Their self-acceptance blows me away. Their example shows me that I am still carrying more shame than I realized. I have not yet learned to love and accept myself quite as much as I thought. I have more to learn.

In addition to assuming themselves for themselves, they challenge the rest of us in a way I've never quite felt able to do. They have an impatience for the world to catch up to them. I see in them a conviction that it's the world that's wrong, not them.

They ask me why we don't have a queer learning community like Umoja, which is focused on empowerment for Black students, or Puente, which focuses on achievement for first-generation and Latinx students. These on campus programs guide the students they support from their arrival at the college through their first year and support them not only academically but as whole beings. Where's the queer learning community?

I don't have a good answer. Truthfully, the idea crossed my mind already, and I told myself, "There's a project I could champion after I get tenure." And here it is, about a year into my career at my college, and a group of impatient queer students wants that space now. And of course they're right. Why wait? We work, and we make it happen. It takes more time to implement than the students want. It's not supported enough at first. It's far from the full vision yet. But it happens.

2018. On a car ride to a conference, I have a conversation with a close colleague who asks: "What's it like to be so 'out'?" What's it like to be so visible? Does it change my relationship with my students? Do I blur the line between my private life and my professional life? I sense in his questions a sense of wonder, bafflement, even. Incredulity mixed with a hint of envy. I fight the urge to protest, to say I'm not really that out, not as much as he thinks; by now, I've assumed my position as the go-to queer prof. But it feels odd to be held up in this way. I feel as if this colleague sees in me a bravery I don't see in myself.

In advanced composition courses I sometimes teach a book called *Covering* by Kenji Yoshino (2007), a gay Asian-American law professor who argues that though we as a society have made civil rights advances to affirm the equality of marginalized peoples, and though in large part we no longer live in a society that enforces the closet on queer people in particular—a society, he points out, that was epitomized by the now obsolete "don't ask, don't tell" policy—we are not quite there yet on LGBTQIA+ rights, or rights for people of color, people with disabilities, women. Some important basic rights are written into law, but for many marginalized groups, we still ask them to "tone it down" a little. To not be too loud, too visible. Exist, feel free to talk about it, but don't play up your difference too much. Succeed by being "professional." Be *neutral*. This toleration for difference combined with an imperative to not be *too* different is what Yoshino calls "covering." To cover is to "tone down a disfavored identity to fit into the mainstream" (p. ix).

Yoshino puts language to something that shapes my whole way of being in the world but which I have struggled to put my finger on. I am not fully there in the room with my students. I am still somehow hiding something, without even really knowing why.

The book itself is a model for how to move beyond covering. Yoshino, a lawyer, presents a legal and social argument, but many of his examples are taken from his own life: his relationship with his father, his history in academia, at work, arguments with boyfriends. These examples sit right next to Supreme Court cases, historical events, and philosophical scenarios. He frames all of his examples as equally serious objects of analytical study. He is academically rigorous and yet so exposed, so fully present in his own book. Part of why I have students read it is to empower them to show up fully as writers. Good writing is not what you think your teacher wants to read. It's not neutral. You don't need to disappear by never saying "I." It's you—all of you—in your words, in your sentences, in your arguments.

2019. Now, thanks to the urging of the QSA students, I'm in the dream position of getting to teach English in a queer learning community. In a unit on queer theory, we read an article by Sandra Bem (1975), a psychologist who studied gender in the 1970s. She focuses on what she calls "androgyny," an old-school term I think would best be translated into modern lingo as "gender nonconforming." Her essential argument is that androgynous people are undervalued and underestimated, pathologized even, when they have, according to her, noted psychological advantages compared to binary men and women.

We wrap up class for the day, and one of the more gregarious students comes up to me to tell me how fascinated he was by the discussion, how much it opened his eyes to possibilities he had never considered. Then he says, "I wish I were like you."

"Like me?"

"Yeah, androgynous, like you."

I'm taken aback. I didn't assign this text as any kind of personal statement. I didn't think it was about me at all. Plus, it was one of those conversations in the classroom that gained momentum on its own, with students responding to one another organically; I didn't see myself as particularly central to the discussion, even. And yet, from where this student stands, me with my loud shirt and dangly earrings at the front of the classroom—what else would we be talking about?

With visibility comes attention, and a lot of work. I start receiving emails from faculty members I don't know, asking questions about resources for queer students or seeking tips to navigate a challenging situation with a queer student. The QSA frequently puts me in touch with queer students who have a problem with a professor. The learning community requires an incredible amount of work—which I do on my own time, since I'm not compensated for this coordination work at first. I am beginning to understand what organizers call "activism fatigue."

I am, of course, not the only queer on campus, and a few of us gather, as we can, to push for changes and growth here and there. Eventually, we form a task force, which comes to be called the Pride Alliance, to organize our efforts and gather more support. Soon we have 20-something members. They say many hands make light work, and it's true that with many hands onboard we are able to make rapid changes. There are concrete and specific advances like our new LGBTQIA+ resources website, the approval we've attained to create a physical Pride Center, the new coordination time for the learning community. And then there are subtler, broader cultural shifts we start to see: Within the space of about a year a critical mass of faculty and staff starts putting pronouns in email signatures and on Zoom; in the face of attacks on trans rights across the country, faculty, Classified Senates, and the student government all endorse a statement of solidarity with trans students, staff, and community members. It's remarkable to see this growing support for the queer community on campus unfold so quickly.

And I feel how visibility is what creates the possibility for this change at a community level. We were—all 20-something members of the Pride Alliance—here before the founding of our group, but somehow we weren't visible to each other. Without visibility, we were alone. When we come together, we can support each other, we see each other, and the campus community sees us. Visibility creates space for community, and community is power.

2021. I'm rethinking my composition course for the queer learning community, Community of Pride. I've taught it twice by now, and it hasn't quite worked. I want this class to be meaningful. There is such an opportunity here to go into territory that is deep and vulnerable with these students. I've seen this in class discussions, where the learning community students really shine, but how to get students to transpose this to writing? To invite them to be vulnerable, present in their whole selves, and still instill in them the importance of a good paragraph, of a clear sentence? I haven't yet cracked it.

I need a new first unit, a reading to help students think about gender and sexuality on one hand, and then think more broadly about how a personal identity can support the foundation of an academic argument. I decide to pick up a copy of a graphic memoir, Gender Queer *by Kobabe (2019), that a colleague recommended to me years ago and I hadn't gotten around to reading.*

Something happens to me as I am reading. A few pages in, my heart is beating in my chest. The memoir traces the history of Kobabe's gender, from moments of dysphoria to moments of euphoria. I see myself in their experience, even if the details are not the same. Most important, though, what I see here is a person who takes their gender seriously—someone who thinks their own experience is important enough to write and illustrate a book about it. A quarter of the way in I think: I could write a memoir like this, if I had the courage; I, too, have experiences that shaped me. When our protagonist, who uses e/em/eir pronouns, figures out that e is nonbinary, that e feels most affirmed by these weird and difficult pronouns, something opens in me. E takes space in the world by assuming a nonnormative identity, by using difficult pronouns, because it feels important to em, important enough to inconvenience others.

Near the end of the book, Kobabe, now out and self-assuming emself as a nonbinary person, describes the experience of leading workshops as an instructor. In one panel e stands at the chalkboard of an empty classroom and thinks, "I wish I didn't fear that my identity is too political for a classroom" (2019, p. 234). After the kids arrive, e asks emself: "I wonder if any of these kids are trans or nonbinary, but don't have the words for it yet? How many of them have never seen a nonbinary adult? Is my silence actually a disservice to them?" (p. 237).

I think, again, about my falling short. A year prior, I impulsively put "he/him/they/them" in my email signature at the start of the semester, with "they/them" as an addendum to my normative male pronouns. This, I see, was a failed compromise. I wanted it to communicate to others my genderqueer-ness, but I also didn't want to ask anyone to make any special effort on my part. And while I succeeded in not bothering anyone with my pronouns—in a year with these pronouns on Zoom and in my email, I didn't once hear anyone refer to me with "they"—I'm not sure what I communicated to others about my gender identity. At this point, I'm not even sure what my gender identity is.

So this is how I queer my pedagogy. In the learning community, we now begin with *Gender Queer*. We also read an open letter from Aimee Stephens (n.d.), the woman who was fired from her job at a funeral parlor after she came out as trans, whose case went all the way to the Supreme Court, which eventually ruled that queer and trans folks are, in fact, protected by the Civil Rights Act. She writes to the employers of America to tell her story and to explain how they can support their trans employees. We see how telling one's own story can contribute in real ways to create a better world for others. Inspired by Kobabe and Stephens, students will write their own open letters to some particular audience, telling a personal story and explaining what others can learn from their experience.

In their papers, students share intimate stories and make powerful arguments. One student uses their story of incarceration and recovery from addiction to make a case to lawmakers to move toward decriminalization of narcotics. A few students write to parents and school administrators about the mental health challenges they faced in school and explain the ways the educational system failed them and must be reformed. Another student reveals how powerful it was to see a queer character in a video game when she was young and urges video game designers to represent more diversity in their games. These essays are remarkably successful, and their power comes from the way they invite students to bring all of themselves to the writing.

Does my own identity play a role in helping my students tell their stories? Surely it does. The fact is that a teacher's presence is, of course, never neutral. Women know this. Teachers of color know this. Disabled teachers know this. Their bodies, their social position, their relative privilege and lack thereof, their power and their vulnerabilities—students of course see all of this. White male teachers might have an easier time convincing themselves of their neutrality, their apparent ability to disappear but it's a fallacy, of course.

All teachers do, as Lecoq said, "place obstacles in [students'] path, so [they] can find [their] own way round them," (as cited in Esslin, 1999) but we are never neutral. And thank goodness. I realize now that a teacher's social position is not a liability, something to hide behind. Sometimes, perhaps, the space we take up is the very obstacle that provides an opportunity for our students to grow.

My fingernails projecting massively on the board behind my head—this opens a door. I think of the student in the room who also painted their nails this weekend and wiped them off before coming to class—they need to see those sparkling nails. Can they draw strength from my boldness? Beyond the queer students, what might the gigglers at the back of the classroom, or those silent boys whose stares I feared, have learned from seeing my sparkling fingernails?

And I am now seeing what Stacey Waite, Kenji Yoshino, Maia Kobabe, and the students of the QSA are teaching me: When I assume my own power and present myself as I am to my students, I can then invite my students to do the same. This, I see now, is how I queer my classroom.

2021. It's the first day of school, the first day of in-person learning since the pandemic began. I look great: I'm wearing a long floral-print dress in black and green, a blue cardigan, blue clogs, subtle (but not too subtle) eye makeup, and periwinkle nails. This time, the nails are probably the least remarkable thing about my appearance.

As I walk past the students and open the door to the classroom, I feel the usual stares of the first day—scrutiny, excitement, fear—which are of course mixed with a dose of something else. A group of seemingly cis male students seem to have clumped in the row of desks by the exit. Near them is a student who is visibly beaming.

As I write my name, my new pronouns "they/them," and the course title on the board, I feel the weight of those stares. I feel, too, something new. Whatever may be going on in the heads of the students behind me, I feel in my bones that their reactions are their own, and that I am, standing here, dressed like this, myself. Their surprise, their discomfort, is part of their journey. And these clogs, these nails, this dress—this is me. I am here in the room, visible. I am somebody. And they are paying attention. We are all here, present, ready to learn from one another.

CONCLUSION

When I first proposed this piece for the Breakthroughs project, I was not sure if it fit the brief. I was interested in tracing a series of small revelations, rather than one decisive "aha" moment. "Coming out" appears to others as a breakthrough, of course, but I hope that I have shown here that it's a process, a long one, that engages our personal lives, professional lives, and innermost selves. For me, the work of finding the outward expression of an inner truth is not an "aha" but an incremental process of becoming.

I hope that my readers, regardless of their own personal identity, see this piece as an invitation to consider their own positionality in the classroom. What does it mean to be a human being who teaches? Who am I? What do I share with my students? What value does my own experience as a human being offer to my students?

At a time in America where "identity politics" and "wokeism" are under attack, especially in education, while simultaneously one in six members of Gen Z identify as LGBTQIA+ (Jones, 2021), it strikes me as vitally important that we offer ourselves with some vulnerability to our students. Our youth, queer or not, need to develop self-love, some inner strength—and some defenses against a world that can sometimes be hostile. And we, as adults, queer or not, have navigated these questions and are equipped to support our students. I have come to understand this kind of support as one of the core responsibilities I have as an educator.

And let's remember, too, that we teachers need to take care of ourselves. What do you need to flourish? Are you covering for your students? Why? Does it help you to cover? Or would it serve you better to bring more of yourself to work with you?

Whatever your answers to these questions—and I am not here to tell you what your answers are!—I hope my piece emboldens you to approach these queries with vulnerability and with honesty, and to embrace the incremental, unfolding breakthroughs you have ahead of you.

RECOMMENDED READING

Nemi Neto, J. (2018). Queer pedagogy: Approaches to inclusive teaching. *Policy Futures in Education, 16*(5), 589–604. https://doi.org/10.1177/1478210317751273

> This article, written by a university language instructor, offers a framework for considering LGBTQIA+ inclusion in the classroom through our use of language and our engagement with textbooks and course materials that offer a cis and heteronormative worldview. It's an especially good primer for anyone new to this topic.

Waite, S. (2017). *Teaching queer: Radical possibilities for writing and knowing.* University of Pittsburgh Press.

> While Waite is focused somewhat narrowly on how to "queer" the pedagogy of the college composition classroom, her approach offers all of us some license to think about how we might invite the self into classroom conversations and how these conversations might lead to creative pedagogical interventions.

Yoshino, K. (2007). *Covering.* Random House.

> This underappreciated book offers a strikingly clear way of thinking about the demands our society places on us to present ourselves inoffensively to others. The book is useful to anyone who has ever felt they needed to "tone it down." Required reading!

About Chapter 11

University of California Berkeley instructor **John Levine** gets caught up in a moment of self-doubt. Should he scrap his tried-and-true reading and writing assignment that asks his students to analyze their reasons for being in college? His worry: "With all the pressures students face upon entering college—living away from home, managing their schedules, making friends—should I really be asking them to question why they were in college in the first place?" His self-critique launches a search for answers to find out once and for all the real effects of these assignments.

At the heart of Levine's breakthrough is a moment every teacher understands: when we suddenly start to lose our footing. What do we do when things seem to be slipping? Levine's first instinct is to drop the course theme he has used for years. But then he has a better idea. Ultimately, he finds out as much about himself as about the young people he taught.

Teacher as Disrupter
When Critical Thinking Gets Personal

John Levine

Engaged pedagogy begins with the assumption that we learn best when
there is an interactive relationship between student and teacher. As leaders
and facilitators, teachers must discover what the students know and what
they need to know. This discovery happens only if teachers are willing to
engage students beyond a surface level.

—hooks, 2010, p. 19

Six weeks into a college course is not the ideal time for an icebreaker activity, but that's what I found myself doing in my first-year composition class.

"Everybody line up along the wall," I instructed the 14 students sitting around the table. "On this end, those who think that the primary purpose of a college education is to gain knowledge. And on the other end, those who think the primary purpose of college is to get a good job."

The two ends of the line grew out of a free-write the students had just done in response to the question "What, in your opinion, is the purpose of college?" The free-write led to a lively discussion out of which emerged multiple reasons for pursuing a postsecondary education. We agreed by consensus that "knowledge" and "job" were the extreme ends of the spectrum.

The theme of my College Writing R1A class is "How and What We Learn," a topic I devised after reading several books and articles about higher education. Since college is one of the things I have in common with my 18- and 19-year-old students, I thought this would be an interesting area to explore with them.

Although the demographics of the class vary from term to term, it's safe to say that each section is diverse, comprising a variety of ethnic and socioeconomic backgrounds. I usually have a number of student athletes and a few international students in the mix. As is true of the general student population at my university, 25% of the class are the first in their family to attend a four-year college.

I have made slight variations in the assigned readings for the course over the three years I focused on "How and What We Learn," but two of the mainstay texts have been *Mindset: The New Psychology of Success* by Carol Dweck (2006), and *Excellent Sheep: The Miseducation of the American Elite and the Way to a Meaningful Life* by William Deresiewicz (2015). *Mindset* proved particularly popular with students in that it has something for everyone: athletes as well as artists, aspiring business majors, and those in or pursuing romantic relationships.

MINDSET

After we read selected chapters from *Mindset*, I introduced the formal writing assignment. Since this was the first paper of the semester and, for many of the students, their first formal writing project since they'd entered college, this assignment drew on a genre I assumed the students were familiar with: the personal narrative, specifically the personal statement they wrote as part of their college application. That piece was, presumably, meaningful to them; there were real stakes involved because the quality of that essay determined whether they were admitted to the college of their choice. But I also wanted to tie the assignment to a reading, so I had them write about themselves using some of the ideas presented by Dweck in *Mindset*. Here's the prompt for Essay #1:

> After reading *Mindset*, construct a personal statement, drawing on the ideas and key terms Dweck uses in her book. Would you say you have what Dweck calls a "fixed mindset," or would you say you have a "growth mindset?" Or are you somewhere in between the two? Are you "fixed" in some areas and "growth" in others? How do you see yourself changing—if at all—after reading Dweck's book? Think about examples that illustrate your self-assessment.

The students enjoyed reading Dweck and I anticipated some interesting responses to the assignment. Here is part of the essay by Harper, a student athlete:

> My life has always been dependent on volleyball. What I eat, how I dress, the way people treat me, and the way I perceive myself are all relevant because of this sport. Looking at my life in regard to volleyball, I recognize my privilege and that my opportunities were unique and extremely lucky. However, after reading Carol S. Dweck's *Mindset: The New Psychology*, I now see that throughout my life I placed value on the wrong things. I looked back seeing the notoriety volleyball gave me for being talented. Now looking back, I see a naïve girl who placed all her worth on her abilities and was swayed by her parents' opinions. In the past, I was influenced by the fixed mindset, praised for my qualification and skill. Today, I see myself as a human being who must fail, take chances and accept change in order to grow.

Because sports had been such a big part of her life, it's no surprise that Harper zeroed in on the chapter "Sports: The Mindset of a Champion." In this passage, she was reflective, using Dweck's ideas to discuss her own development as she recognized the limitations of her fixed mindset, and suggests that she was beginning to adopt more of a growth mindset.

Another student, Sebastian, linked his mindset to his development as a writer. He began by explaining that he bought into the implicit bias that men are good at math and science while women excel in the humanities. He first quotes Dweck: "When stereotypes are evoked, they fill people's minds with distracting thoughts. . . . People usually aren't aware of it" (p. 75). Sebastian responded:

> I have always scored better on math than English. But it is very unlikely that there has always been a discrepancy between both subjects since they are taught at the same time and pace. My only explanation for this is embracing stereotypes. I was taught men like math and science while women like liberal arts.

Another student, Sandotin, focused on the chapter "Relationships: Mindsets in Love (or Not)." His essay began:

> Imagine your heart beating as fast as the sound of a horse galloping! Imagine happiness and joy as the highlights of your day-to-day life! Imagine that at the mere sight of your beloved, all your worries suddenly fade off! Those emotions are what I felt at the time I was involved in several romantic relationships. According to Carol Dweck, author of *Mindset: The New Psychology of Success,* this contentment is the immediate offshoots of having exclusively a growth mindset in love. Likewise, Dweck insists that partners can improve their relationship and similarly grow as individuals through perpetual determination and hard work. Should a person have a fixed mindset or a growth mindset in love? I wonder. It seems to me that romantic loves based on the idea of growth mindset do not necessarily guarantee a successful relationship; in the case of breakups, a growth-mindset-based relationship significantly prevents a person's pursuit of self-reliance. Consequently, I advocate for a more fixed mindset than a growth one in love.

An international student from the Ivory Coast on a full-ride scholarship, Sandotin, I came to discover, was going through a major personal transformation that semester. Looking back, I recognize that his decision to focus on his past romances was a way of sidestepping looking at his current confusion about his education. His flowery prose was not the writing usually produced by students on a STEM-oriented trajectory, yet Sandotin had already declared his civil engineering major in his first semester. Did his writing style belie his vocational aim? Was he a humanities major who had been misdirected?

During one of our individual conferences, Sandotin shared with me that he was, for the first time, thinking deeply about the educational path he had chosen. He didn't offer any specifics about his contemplative state, and I didn't press him for details. It was at that point that I wondered if my choice of theme for the course was, perhaps, inconsiderate. With all the pressures students face upon entering college—living away from home, managing their schedules, making friends—should I really be asking them to question why they were in college in the first place?

Nancy Sommers (1980) in her seminal journal article, "Revision Strategies of Student Writers and Experienced Adult Writers," proposes that "good writing disturbs: it creates dissonance" (p. 387). While I agreed with Sommers's assessment, I had to wonder if I was forcing my students into an existential dissonance they weren't yet ready to face. Good writing may disturb, but should good *writing instruction* also disturb? Who was I to shake up these promising young minds? What right did I have to challenge their—and, in many cases, their families'—ideas about the purpose of college? Presumably, many of these students were at the university as a result of their fixed mindset—because of their dogged determination to get good grades, high test scores, and to participate in multiple community and extracurricular activities—the very formula that paved the way to their admission to our elite educational institution.

EXCELLENT SHEEP

After they submitted their *Mindset* papers and while I was reading and grading them, we moved on to the next text, William Deresiewicz's *Excellent Sheep*. Deresiewicz (2015) takes a candid—though admittedly provocative—look at the current state of American higher education. He pulls no punches when he writes that, "The purpose of college . . . is to turn adolescents into adults. . . . That is the true education: accept no substitutes. The idea that we should take the first four years of young adulthood and devote them to career preparation alone, neglecting every other part of life, is nothing short of an obscenity" (p. 87).

Before moving onto the *Excellent Sheep* writing assignment, I asked the students to reflect on Deresiewicz's ideas in an informal reader-response format. Sandotin wrote:

> I strongly agree with the position of William Deresiewicz about the idea that college is a place where a person needs to battle while confronted with his own self. College is about getting an education in order for a person to pursue a meaningful life based on his own desire and his own choice. The person should use his own lenses to his dream in defining what is the meaning of his own life. I will say, I am exhausted of solving math equations over and over again. I am

tired of doing the same thing, while even not being sure of what I want to do or what I want to pursue in my life. I feel totally trapped in [the] middle of a river. Which side should I go to? I do not know. To be totally honest, I am in conflict with my own being. Should I follow what I am interested about or should I follow the path to get more money? In other words, should I create my own path or [be] part of the *doxa* (p. 80). But even though I decide to follow my own passion, I still lack the moral courage to pursue it.

Reading Sandotin's reflection at that point gave me pause. Did reading and writing about *Excellent Sheep* cause him to "feel totally trapped?" Didn't he have enough on his plate without my prompting him to follow his bliss? Was I overstepping my bounds as an instructor?

Not every student took such a deep dive. Here was Harper's response:

I feel I am at a "point of inflection" right now in my life because everyone around me has an idea of what they want to major in/do with their lives, and I don't. Deresiewicz addresses something very influential to me stating, "You won't be able to recognize the things you really care about until you have released your grip on all the things that you've been taught to care about" (p. 90). This really resonates with me because I hope I have the courage to brush off what people tell me to do and instead listen to myself. I am my greatest resource, and sometimes it's hard to remember that. I have always wanted to be a teacher but have always been discouraged from pursuing it because of the low pay. It makes me question my own worth, wondering if maybe I am selling myself short. I know these next few years will be tough, but if I listen to my gut instinct, things will work out. Life is a marathon not a race and I have to be comfortable trusting the process.

I'm somewhat embarrassed to admit that I was comforted by Harper's declaration that she "always wanted to be a teacher," despite "the low pay." She took Deresiewicz's advice not as a disruptive call to action, but as a reminder to trust her sense of self.

Lily, an international student from Shenzhen, China, was not so quick to accept Deresiewicz's claims. She wrote:

My feelings on the author's lines are rather mixed. I do support his position that college should teach students to think differently and profoundly [about] the world and themselves, and it's preferable to invent life paths by pursuing things that people enjoy doing for their own sake. However, I find his arguments and suggestions distant and radical from time to time, or in other words, not practical and convincing enough for readers to follow. . . . I could see the reason why Deresiewicz is referring to all the extreme and radical examples . . . and I have to admit they're quite impressive, throwing me to carefully deliberate my own mindsets. Nonetheless, if he could go down to earth earlier in his article, or [offer] more practical suggestions to readers, it may be more helpful for us to take up his advice, and really try to "take time off" from college.

Lily politely listened to what Deresiewicz had to say, but then challenged him to get real, to offer "more practical suggestions" about the best use of an expensive college education.

In his reader response, Sebastian took Deresiewicz to task on the author's limited view of postsecondary education. Deresiewicz's frame of reference was his time as a student at Columbia and as a professor at Yale. Sebastian wrote:

> If the purpose of higher education was only to teach people how to think, all colleges would be equal in the eyes of employers and students. But this is not the truth. There are community colleges, UCs, and CSUs in California. Each is a different prestige and quality of education. . . . This leads me to believe that the purpose of higher education is verification of knowledge and skill.

Sebastian was exercising critical thinking in the best sense: He was taking an author's ideas, questioning them, and building upon them.

My prompt for the next paper asked the class to combine Deresiewicz's ideas with those of a selected shorter ancillary text they'd read in the class. Most of these short texts are opinion pieces from the *New York Times*. Many students gravitated to a piece by Nathan Gebhard (2015), titled "Four Steps to Choosing a College Major," in which Gebhard presents a practical approach, balancing pursuing an interest with making a living. "Your ultimate goal," my assignment sheet read, "is to synthesize the ideas of other writers and build a discussion about a specific topic related to how we think and learn." Here are excerpts from students' final drafts.

Harper:

> There needs to be a cultural shift among college students to focus more so on interest-based learning rather than what is deemed "the path to success." Students need to follow what they and only they are interested in and disregard any predisposed path someone else has told them to follow. In Gebhard's article, he poses a list presenting four tips to help choose a college major. The title of his first step in bold print lists, "Separate your goals from other people's goals for you" (Gebhard). With other people's voices drowning out your own how are you ever supposed to find what you are passionate about? Outside influences will always be present, in a lot of cases, distracting you from achieving your goals. Deresiewicz mentions the importance of letting what's not important to you go, in order to target what's most meaningful to you by writing, "You won't be able to recognize the things you really care about until you have released your grip on all the things that you've been taught to care about" (p. 90).

It's not surprising that Harper gravitated to this particular theory, as it coincided with the idea she presented in her *Mindset* essay about prioritizing her parents' wishes over her own. But now I wondered if Harper was allowing her mindset to evolve, or if she was simply reiterating the same ideas about trusting one's gut rather than being influenced by others. Lily concluded her *Excellent Sheep* essay with the following:

> As a student beginning to worry about choosing a proper major and career from high school, I was greatly relieved by reading the work of Gebhard and Deresiewicz. Now I believe what I need to do is simply follow and nurture my interest, stay open to opportunities, think deeply and frequently about myself and the world, and actively prepare for my career once I feel the inner compulsion. Thanks to Gebhard and Deresiewicz, my college life has fundamentally changed in a positive way, and I can't be more grateful for the two insightful writers.

Lily surprised me; she was more equivocal in her final paper than she had been in her previous writing. She took comfort in Deresiewicz's and Gebhard's advice to follow her interest. Then again, she was more confident than other students about her academic path. She was saying, essentially, "Thanks, Gebhard and Deresiewicz, but I've got this under control."

Sandotin quoted Deresiewicz and then weaved in his own story:

> "There is something that's a great deal more important than parental approval: learning to do without it. That's what it means to become an adult" (Deresiewicz, 2015, p. 121; Ch. 6). Throughout those words, the author insists that adulthood is the disregard of parental approval and help upon making our college decision. Oppositely to this claim, I do gather that there is more to this freedom of adulthood. It isn't only about following what you want, but rather, to borrow some words from Gebhard, it is a "meandering process of critical thinking and a winding process of [weighing] different points of view, yours and your parents," and being the only one to come up with meaningful resolutions. In fact, correlating adulthood and refutation of parents' opinions, as Deresiewicz suggests, is a mistake that I can relate to. Being at the University of California, Berkeley has been difficult as the cultural adjustment was a struggle. During the first two months, I restricted myself from sharing my setbacks with my parents, having in mind that I could solve them by myself. On Sunday morning, after breaking down, due to anxiety resulting from my college major and social life, I finally made the decision to get my parents involved in my daily struggles. What happened was phenomenal: My father reminded me of the countless difficulties I overcame, [as a non-English speaker] trying to adjust to my life in South Africa, two years before coming to Cal. He cheered me up and he did reassure me that I could go through the challenges I was facing here. It was indeed meaningful to share my feelings with my parents because from interacting with them, I

was able to look, on my own, for other ways to improve my time at this place. In light of all this, adulthood is a characteristic that [requires one's] ability to gather confidence from parents in order to thrive on their own.

It was at that point, after reading Sandotin's essay and meeting with him in conference, that I again questioned myself. I had been a middling student in college; I was late to choose a major and only decided on English because I had acquired enough credits to satisfy the major. If someone had asked me when I was 18 what the purpose of college was, I would have been hard-pressed to come up with an answer. After graduating, I held a variety of jobs and decided to go to graduate school at age 34 because I still had no idea what I wanted to be when I grew up. So why was I now subjecting my students to this mental torture? Perhaps it was because I was just now, in middle age, asking myself, why college?

By the end of that semester, I decided to retire the course theme because, I told myself, it was time to shake things up and choose a new theme (I went with the more anodyne "telling stories" theme). But in retrospect, it was the fear that I was being irresponsible in challenging these young people to question their reasons for being in college. While I won't dispute Socrates's idea that the unexamined life is not worth living, these students had plenty of time to examine their lives after graduation, or at least after their freshman year in college.

HARPER, SEBASTIAN, LILY, AND SANDOTIN: WHERE ARE THEY NOW?

The plight of first-year college composition instructors is that we have the privilege of ushering students into the academic universe, but we seldom find out where they land. Writing this essay gave me the motivation to see where some of these students were. Three of them, Lily, Sebastian, and Harper are about to graduate from college. I contacted them by email to find out what major they chose, how they think they've changed since their first year, and what they remember from our writing class.

Harper is a media studies major with a minor in conservation resource studies. "To be completely candid," she explains, "I chose this major because I had no idea what I wanted to major in, I knew older people from my team who were in the major, and I thought the major was going to be interdisciplinary, exposing me to different things." As far as what she now thinks the purpose of college is, she wrote:

I have learned a lot of history and theories and not a lot of applicable things that I feel will propel me in my life after college. I feel ready for life after college because I am confident in my abilities as a person to be adaptable and resilient, but I don't feel prepared intellectually. But once again, I think the most valuable thing I have gotten from college hasn't been the Berkeley education, but it's been the experiences I've made, the friendships I've fostered, and the hard, gritty challenges I've overcome. Unfortunately, I think the purpose of college is now too focused on the degree rather than focusing on being uncomfortable, taking risks, failing, and learning to get back up and try again.

Sebastian is a data science major with an emphasis in cognition. He explained:

I think I have changed since I took [your class]. I have been able to push myself in what I learn, even if the class is tedious and difficult. I enjoy the classes for the content when I get into it, even if my grade does not reflect my enjoyment for the class. I am more willing to try new things if I am interested in it because failure is part of the cycle of learning and the class really put that into perspective. Now, just because I am not good at something does not mean I should give up or try to find an easier route. That lesson was first taught by your class but I did not fully accept it until I failed Spanish 2 when the pandemic first hit. If anything, I have become a more resilient person.

Lily is a double major: computer science and molecular and cell biology. She thinks she has changed fundamentally since her first year:

I've learned to accept myself, accept all my imperfections and "dumb" mistakes. I've also learned to collaborate more with friends and express love to people around. I'm still anxious sometimes due to academic pressure, but much less frequently, and life has become much happier with the new attitude. . . . I'd say the purpose of college is to accept our true selves, learn about our mental needs deep inside, and learn to communicate and work with people.

Once again, Lily surprised me. I had pegged her as a single-minded (though double-majored) student, devoted to her fixed mindset of academic success. If she was anxious or worried about her imperfections during her first year, I was not aware.

Unlike the others, Sandotin was further along on his path. He had taken my class two years before the other three and had already completed his undergraduate studies. After getting his bachelor's degree in civil engineering, he returned to Berkeley as a graduate student in civil and environmental engineering with a focus on structural engineering. He doesn't recall what I remembered as his existential crisis. His memories of that first year of college were more the linguistic obstacles he faced as a nonnative speaker of English. When I asked him if he thought that challenging first year students to question their reasons for being in college was wrong, he replied:

I'd say it wasn't wrong. When I came into Berkeley I came in as an architect; that's how I was admitted. Even before taking the class, I had the thought of going into the civil engineering field, which is more technically oriented—the physics of building—while architects focus on the design of buildings. I would say the class made me really question the reason I wanted to do that. And it helped me make a decision I already wanted to make—I would say, to support that decision. . . . If anything, if you have a trajectory in mind, when those questions come, they can test that devotion and see if that's something you are really committed to. . . . All the questions we developed during the class really reinforced that desire of what I really wanted to do.

And so, my fear about Sandotin abandoning civil engineering to become an impoverished poet was just a fantasy—*my fantasy*. Although he may have been wrestling with what he was going to do, he, like so many of my students, was resilient.

I now realize that I was arrogant in thinking that I had the power to single-handedly steer these inquisitive minds off course. Carol Dweck would say I had a fixed mindset when it comes to teaching; I believed that I have far more influence than I actually have. The good news: I've learned from this experience. And now, if and when I return to my "How and What We Learn" course theme, I can be confident that students can handle the challenge of questioning their academic pathways. In fact, they *should* question them. And I should help them in every way I can.

CONCLUSION

As good teachers, inevitably, at some point we doubt ourselves. If we didn't periodically question our practice, we wouldn't be effective educators. It was my self-doubt that inspired me to write this essay. But as I think about the conclusion I came to, and the resulting action of abandoning my course theme, I wonder if I went too far. (Wait a minute. Now I'm doubting my self-doubt.) I realize I should have the courage of my convictions: I should give my "How and What We Learn" theme another spin. After all, my college writing students—at least the four profiled here—were not traumatized. And you might even say that they experienced a breakthrough in my class, each in their own way.

Was my class instrumental in their process of self-discovery? Yes. But so were their many other college encounters inside and outside the classroom. Throughout their college years, these students learned some fundamental truths about themselves, as evidenced by their reflections about our class. Harper went from hoping to "have the courage to brush off what people tell me to do and instead listen to myself," to feeling "ready for life after college," bolstered by "the experiences I've made, the friendships I've fostered, and the hard, gritty challenges I've overcome." During his first year, Sebastian felt certain that "the purpose of higher education is verification of knowledge and skill." Three years later, he concluded: "I am more willing to try new things . . . because failure is part of the cycle of learning." And Sandotin, well along in his graduate studies, reflected that the struggles he faced that first year of college "reinforced that desire of what I really want to do."

My own breakthrough came to me, not in the classroom, not even as I sat at my desk a few years later, beginning to write this essay. My discovery came through the process of writing and rewriting this piece—as I figured out what it all means. And I'm sure this essay is not the final word. But besides recognizing what little effect my teaching has on my students' understanding of who they are, I've also come to appreciate the importance of writing as a means of discovery. And the writing doesn't have to be published—though I encourage you to share your own breakthroughs with your fellow educators. Write for yourself. Practice what you preach. Share your writing with your students as you ask them to share theirs with you. Who knows what discoveries you—and they—will make?

RECOMMENDED READING

Caplan, B. (2018, January). The world might be better off without college for everyone. *The Atlantic.*

> This essay shines a light on the disconnect between what students are taught in college courses and the knowledge they need to function in society.

Fremont High School Students. (2022, September 1). What grown-ups don't understand about school. *The New York Times.* https://www.nytimes.com/2022/09/01/opinion/us-high-school-oakland.html

> As the title suggests, this essay provides a snapshot of what school means to a group of (Oakland) high school students—recommended for teachers and parents.

hooks, b. (2010). *Teaching critical thinking: Practical wisdom.* Routledge.

> Writer and educator bell hooks was always striving to become a more effective teacher. Her ideas are aspirational but also reasonable.

Mansharamani, V. (2022, June 15). Harvard lecturer: 'No specific skill will get you ahead in the future'—but this 'way of thinking' will. https://www.cnbc.com/2020/06/15/harvard-yale-researcher-future-success-is-not-a-specific-skill-its-a-type-of-thinking.html

> This piece challenges the prevailing notion that general knowledge is of little value in our technology-driven world.

Ray, B. (2019, October 21). How to help young people transition into adulthood. *Greater Good.* https://greatergood.berkeley.edu/article/item/how_to_help_young_people_transition_into_adulthood

> Rites of passage into becoming adults need a reboot. This article offers a three-step approach to helping students find their way.

About Chapter 12

In her retrospective vignettes about her teaching career, high school teacher **Rebekah Caplan** reflects on the energy and momentum that carries her and her students to test the limits of what's possible. In stories like "The Show Not Tell Years," Caplan captures the specifics of her work, the hum of a student-centered classroom, and the spirit of continuing discovery.

What characterizes Caplan's breakthroughs is her attention to her students' work, their understandings, even their offhand comments, all of which she uses to craft their next writing experiences, their next mutual breakthroughs. In classrooms from California to Kuwait to Shanghai, Caplan sets a high bar for engagement. "Without realizing it at the time, I was entering the world of inquiry-driven practice, seizing on students' questions . . . pushing us all into spaces of reflection and analysis."

CHAPTER 12

From Breakthroughs to Through Lines
Navigating the Crosswinds of Practice

Rebekah Caplan

An invitation to a conversation about breakthroughs in teaching sets me spinning. With encouragement to join in and tell a good tale, I can't wait to get going and to contribute. But predictably, I become stalled. There is so much to wade through: the crosswinds of practice, the ebbs and flows of theory, the technological blitz overtaking the senses.

In this state of mind, I confess turning to a particular text to help me sift through the maze of moments of a teaching lifetime.

I take my inspiration from celebrated *New Yorker* journalist Janet Malcolm and her publication, *Forty-one False Starts: Essays on Artists and Writers* (2013) and, in particular, the first essay of the collection, "Forty-One False Starts" (2014), which portrays David Salle, a prominent New York artist from the 1980s.

David Salle is known for his postmodern, neo-Expressionist style—his collage-like artwork that layers disparate images in different modes and mediums. Though readers may or may not know of David Salle, my fascination with the text is less about Salle and more about how Malcolm approaches the journalistic task, writing in fits-and-starts, trying *forty-one* possible beginnings to capture a complicated figure, numbering her starts as she goes.

In fact, Malcolm's free-spirited structural design becomes a kind of *through line* for how she captures David Salle. It's art mimicking art here. It's meta. That's one way you get a grip on the artist in the form of a mosaic, where all entry points count.

If the writer started here or there, what difference might it make for what might follow? Maybe no difference at all.

And the parallel for my own writing dilemma: What if I revealed this teaching moment or that teaching moment as they occur to me? Where would telling a few tales here and there lead me in offering perhaps a different kind of breakthrough story reflecting a lifetime of teaching? Might there be breakthroughs that lead to a through line or two?

And so I'm off, musing through the moments that come to mind.

WALLPAPERING CLASSROOM SPACES

This writing task gets students moving at the start of a school year—in fact, it's a kind of assessment, but they don't think of it that way:

> Compose a mimic for this advice Russian author, Anton Chekhov, is said to have offered his brother who aspired to become a writer: "Don't tell me the moon is shining; show me the glint of light on broken glass" (Yarmolinsky, 1954, p. 14).

Student mimics, Jian Ping High School, Shanghai, China:

> *Don't tell me water is important to humans; show me what will happen if we run out of it.*

> *Don't tell me Voldemort is evil; show me how much he wants Harry Potter to die.*

> *Don't tell me sun has rised, show me the heat of sunshine wakes up the sleeping kid on his bed.*

Now imagine, if you will, students wallpapering space next to the chalkboard with sentence-length imitations such as these, written on colorful king-sized sticky notes. The task is intended to reveal to what extent students can exchange a generality for a single detail—an aspect of my practice I am devoted to addressing. The wallpapering also builds a sense of community and individual voice and encourages playfulness as we read our versions aloud.

We maintain this space as a reference point so we can revisit early interpretations of Chekhov's counsel and add and adjust as we think about the impact of elaboration for composing in different genres.

THE SHOW NOT TELL YEARS

I have an argument about my practice, straight up, borne from several breakthroughs over the years. It's a kind of mantra: *Students need multiple opportunities to practice new concepts in familiar contexts.*

I did not compose this statement. A presenter at a professional development workshop I once attended suggested this important principle of EL practice, and I never forgot it. "Bingo," I said to myself. Those words seemed profound to me at the time because they gave me a way to capsulize an aspect of my practice I deeply believed in but never had the precision to say in just that way.

I guess I came to this belief somewhat intuitively in my early years of teaching. I had a fuzzy notion about the value of repeated "practice" in "familiar contexts" as I drew on my drama background to teach writing. In my undergrad classes as a dramatic arts major, improvisational warm-ups were stepping stones for taking on more complicated roles with confidence.

Warm-ups called upon young actors to draw on everyday experiences to build their capacity for being real, to convince audiences they were "really feeling it" in order to come across believably in preparation for more extensive roles. Without my realizing it at first, the practice of improvisation carried over into my practice for developing writer skill with elaboration, especially because students, in most cases, wrote in sweeping generalizations.

Take the Chekhov mimics composed early in the year. Most students appreciate Chekhov's example, but only a few actually demonstrate the specificity he is advocating, as in: "Don't tell me sun has risen, show me the heat of sunshine wakes up the sleeping kid on his bed." This is a rendition composed by an English learner who, though not grammatically fluent, imitates Chekhov's example aptly.

So, in the interest of cultivating a mindset toward appreciation of detail, I invented a little exercise which I made up without much forethought, just to have fun really, but I also wondered whether "repeated practice in familiar contexts" (though I didn't have those words at the time) would build writer fluency, support English learners' language growth, and expand writers' capacity to elaborate meaningfully, no matter the genre.

Extending the Chekhov challenge, I would assign a "telling idea": *The room was a mess; The game was a close one; She is artistic; I was gobsmacked*—maybe three workouts a week. Students were called upon to "show" the idea in a paragraph or two (no more) and get it across in any way that made sense to them. That was the improv part. The particular twist on the exercise was *not* to use the telling sentence in the writing at all—to resist the temptation to start off with a topic sentence, and instead, jump in and unfold the details.

This calisthenic, if you will, was akin to playing charades. You get a little slip of paper with a quote or saying, and you have to "act it out" so your team members get it without directly revealing what's on the paper.

This was a game students could embrace. And even better, as time went on, a writers' community grew because students couldn't wait to see how other students "showed" the same idea. Distinct voices blossomed from diverse perspectives, and multilingual learners howled when they heard peers use home languages interspersed with English.

Sometimes this happened: "Hey, I have a good one for tomorrow. *Rico G. is paranoid!* Let's write about that!" (in reference to a classmate's perfectionist tendencies).

Cheers went up, with some students writing before the bell rang.

Fear not. Rico G. was a beloved and well-known campus figure who students very much admired.

The next day, after his classmates read their versions of Rico's meticulousness, Rico practically got a standing ovation when he detailed the fascination he had with perfection, which in the end, fascinated his readers.

Breakthrough. Students took the reins when I wasn't looking, and our journey into literary analysis went up a notch as they challenged each other to defend a character interpretation.

Students began to take over the class more and more in this way as content creators— certainly not all of them, nor every class, but for the most part, student initiative, student writing, and student voice were trending.

Once, when assigning the sentence *I was gobsmacked*—an expression that clearly turned out to be outdated—one student shouted, "I can't even . . ." as if to say, "That is so last century."

Okay, so what about this sentence: *I can't even . . .*

THE PIZZA TASTED GOOD

There's a similar breakthrough I call *the pizza moment.* The writing grew from a randomly assigned sentence, *The pizza tasted good.*

As it turned out, one writer described nothing about particular ingredients of a particular pizza as most students had done, but instead, wrote about a never-to-be-forgotten getaway, reuniting with a beloved older brother who had moved away and whom she hadn't seen in quite a while. The writer centered on showing all the meaningful activities the two engaged in on one particular day, and it wasn't until the last line that she got to a pizza:

> *The stringy pizza we had purchased for lunch brought childish grins to our faces, and through the warm silence we both knew that pizza had never tasted so good* (as quoted in Caplan, 1984, p. 172).

"That was really different," her response partner offered after the writer read her piece aloud.

"What do you mean by different?" I pushed.

"Well, you know, most of us wrote about tomato sauce and cheese or pepperoni and crusts, but she didn't even get to a pizza until the last sentence. Is that okay? Does that *show* that the pizza tasted good?"

"What do the rest of you think?"

INTERMISSION

Full transparency. I was gobsmacked (apologies to my students) by this writer's elaboration because she reminded me of a universal truth about the pleasures of food that I hadn't thought of myself when I randomly came up with that telling sentence. But I kept quiet, suppressing my glee, and indulged a class debate.

Some students clearly experienced an aha moment for how context and conditions might "make something taste good." As one student put it, "You could be backpacking and hiking all day on a steep mountain trail, and, when you finally set up evening camp, a can of beans tastes *so good*. But I'm not really looking forward to opening a can of beans for dinner tonight."

Others had different opinions, claiming the writer had broken the rules. "I thought we're not supposed to say, 'the pizza tasted good' in the description."

Still holding my excitement at bay . . .

Some students remained in a "follow the rules" mindset—a question of fairness, really—while others had a few doors open as this writer tested the limit of a rule. My breakthrough moment came when, instead of pronouncing a verdict one way or another I decided to let questions hang in the air. In that moment I felt a lecture coming on to defend the pizza alternative—you know, with a *Yes, but don't you see that . . . ? Don't you get it? . . . Didn't you ever . . .?* But responding in that way would have only reinforced *the teacher* as *always right*.

Instead, I suggested we take on the idea of "making something different"—a lesson in *context* really—to see what happens, what might qualify for effective evidence for a common idea. Without this turning point, I don't know whether I would have ever moved writers to this new way of approaching our elaborative exercises.

"What are other ways we might convey an everyday idea? Let's see what happens," I counseled, and of course, some students went to town.

Without my realizing it at the time, I was entering the world of inquiry-driven practice, seizing on students' questions in moments of engagement and pushing us all into spaces of increased reflection and analysis.

WHAT MAKES SOMETHING EPIC?

In recent teaching at the American School of Kuwait, I hoped a teachable moment might happen when one writer or another might elaborate a common idea uniquely. And it happened with "Joseph's" emoji poem, and how students thought the approach *epic*—their word. So right then and there, we decided to inaugurate "an epic board," reserved only for writing that most of us agreed was off-the-charts. The identification of "we know it when we see it" deserved a special kind of honor, but not without an obligation to consider *why* a particular piece was worthy.

We didn't overdo it though, and we didn't use rubrics. We seemed to know that epic writing might be a kind of rare bird, so we were sparing and selective in our nominations.

Here's a nomination from a writing group—an introduction to a personal essay titled, "Red-Brick Walls," that one of the writing group members had drafted:

> *My mind is surrounded by The Great Wall of China, the walls of Constantinople, that for a long time, nobody could penetrate. They rise up past the moon and stars, consuming the stone whole. This process is unconscious, each of these bricks are someone I'm trying to keep out. Letting someone in, I play a life-sized Jenga, plucking out a single brick, allowing them to worm their way in.*

A representative from the writing group scribbled the text on a sticky-note and rushed to post it on the epic board opposite the wallpaper with the Chekhov mimics. The defense? The group appreciated how the writer had worked with expanding an earlier "telling idea," as in *I put up walls around myself*, and converted the general to a metaphoric depiction—the telling-to-showing workouts now serving as a potent revision tool. They said it was the writer's imagery showing the severity of her shyness that made the text deserving of the epic honor.

"So, as long as a writer uses imagery, the writing qualifies for the epic board?"

I recognized, of course, how their reader analysis was at a telling and not a showing level which of course happens all the time when readers "know it when they see it"; it's sort of on the tips of their tongues, but they can't quite explain it.

And it's not only students who are in the mire, trying to nail what it is in a passage that turns heads. It's their teacher, too, who, in the moment, may hem and haw to find a precise explanation.

In fact, we need each other. This is not a quiz. It's our shared interest in unraveling meaning. That's the breakthrough: The lines between teacher and students blur.

"So . . . This is the critical reading challenge before us. What is it about these images that stuns us so much? What makes the imagery qualify for epic-level? That's our inquiry.

"What about The Great Wall of China? The walls of Constantinople? A Jenga game? What do we think of when we see these walls in our mind's eye? What do we feel?"

A fortress. Something permanent. Something protective and so strong it can't be knocked down. The writer is *seriously* shy.

And off they went, continuing with associations. In the end, students came to articulate how they appreciated the contrast of these historic, impenetrable walls with the more contemporary, interactive walls of a Jenga game. The image of a Jenga *move* illustrates a ray of light for breaking out of a shell.

We feel the writer's inner struggle deeply because of the unexpected, even surprising images she chooses to make us feel what she feels.

So we record our analysis on another sticky note and affix our words next to the passage of honor on the epic board. *Students and their teacher need multiple opportunities to practice "articulating" how unique renderings succeed in familiar contexts.*

In short, I would like to suggest that student texts (in early and recent teaching) become part of the literary canon for the course because students are drawn to each other's ideas as especially relevant, and because they want to stop and talk a lot about heart-stopping interpretations. Students find themselves talking about each other's texts as if we're talking about the works of James Baldwin or the poetry of Sarah Kay. As time goes on, some students find themselves imitating each other or quoting from each other, resisting writing about familiar ideas in simplistic ways.

So here is a *through line* for these breakthrough episodes when student text unexpectedly takes center stage: *Student writing is the "accidental literary canon" of my practice.*

THE *COCKTAIL* STORY

One year I asked my principal to give me the most unreachable, recalcitrant students because I intended to prove that if you treat disinterested students as if they know things, believing they are as advanced as, let's say, your AP-qualifying students, they will show just how advanced they are.

At the time, maybe 10 years into my practice, I saw myself as an approachable teacher, a teacher armed with lessons I was always ready to alter to make things relevant for a new crop of learners. My assignments often prompted students to say, "We never did this in any of our other English classes. This is fresh."

So, I was ready for any protests, sarcasm, whining.

But, in this particular year, the principal more than came through in offering me what I had asked for. These students disrespected everything I was about.

Beyond the typical "Why do we even have to do this?" they decided to just fully ignore me by rearranging their seating so they wouldn't have to face me. When, on one bold occasion, I asked a student to "please turn around," he responded over his shoulder—back still turned south—"I'm *not* turned around."

Sounds like one of those high school movies they make every few years about a teacher struggling to connect with unfazed and defiant youth. But, for a young teacher, it's a timeless story worth telling, no matter the cliché—a *breakthrough* story, a rite of passage, maybe.

So, in this case, I set aside all lessons, pulling up a chair for a cozy talk, a *fireside chat*, inviting us to have a frank and honest conversation, no holds barred.

But sincerity made little headway—nor did humoring or "healing sessions" with the school counselor. The principal's talk was a dud, and parent intervention, a laughing stock.

In a moment of complete resignation, complete depletion—a moment of *calm*, actually—I turned to this defiant cast of characters one day and posed: "Just tell me one thing you would be willing to do in this class. Just one thing, and I'll do it."

There was a profound moment of silence, a look in students' eyes of incredulity.

Did I really mean it? Was I actually putting the ball in their court?

One of the ring leaders signaled for others to huddle. And, in about two minutes they had a plan, a request, and actually faced forward for a change.

"You know what we want? We want you to show the movie *Cocktail* with Tom Cruise."

"DONE," I said, without thinking twice and without even knowing what the movie was about. Frankly, I didn't care to know whether *Cocktail* would be objectionable and would require permission forms sent home.

I just did it.

And so, over a period of four days, in the lights-down setting of classroom viewing, I watched in the shadows while students propped their feet on desks, belly-laughed at all the great moments (imaginary popcorn popping into mouths).

On the final day of viewing when the lights went up, with laughter reverberating and abounding, I couldn't believe what came out of my mouth. It's not like I planned what I had to say.

"I don't get it. What is it about this film that is so great?

"You don't get it? You don't get it? Hah. She doesn't get it."

"Okay. I showed this movie because you asked. Now, it's your turn to do something for me. Kindly take out a sheet of paper and inform me what it is that impresses you so much. What's the point?"

And they did it. For a few extended minutes, I heard only the scribbling of pencils across paper.

That night I read their writing and never got to sleep. They all had a lot to say. I knew they would probably relish reading each other's thoughts, so I madly typed up a few lines from each paper, preparing a handout of quotes but leaving writer's names off. The next day I distributed the interpretations, and we read them aloud.

Some recounted the plot line: beginning, middle, end; one appreciated a "chasing dreams" theme, remarking how some dreams come true while others are never realized; another was drawn to a "rags to riches" tale; another wrote about unrequited love; another wrote about the challenges of growing up and having to face life's realities; several commented on the bar scenes and the wild crazy antics which were the best part of the film; one writer expressed a very strong opinion about how the plot made girls out to be "playthings."

When the reading rounds were over, students looked up. They looked at me, and I looked at them. What might be next? What might I say?

Cautious not to be overly enthusiastic (I think they already knew we were onto something), I calmly, if not delicately, said next: "Let's keep going. Let's do more of this."

That's the *breakthrough* moment: Students had become curators of our content.

Almost right away, I sensed a kind of liberation and maybe, a new-found trust as we completed whole essays about *Cocktail*.

I took a risk by deciding then and there we would read *The Great Gatsby* because I saw it at that instant: the opportunity to connect some dots between their impressions of *Cocktail* and questions surrounding The American Dream.

We continued the practice of writing these little interpretations as we plowed through Fitzgerald. Various ideas led us into conversations about idealized visions of happiness, materialism; wealth in terms of White privilege; of women depicted as "playthings," or, as one student suggested in an end-of-class quick write: "as beautiful airheads without any brains," referencing Daisy Buchanan and Jordan Baker sitting on a couch as they were, "buoyed up as though upon an anchored balloon" (p. 8).

As we forged ahead, students continued writing their brief interpretations. Sometimes I typed them up as I had done with *Cocktail*; other times, we just read them aloud spontaneously. Gradually, the idea of a shattered American Dream emerged more strikingly to them. With that, they especially liked to talk about how the story of *Gatsby* might be different if the women were telling the tale, and they were particularly interested in what Myrtle Wilson might have had to say.

The breakthrough with that wayward class and the story from *Cocktail*-to-*Gatsby* has lasted a teaching lifetime. I could never reproduce this exact experience again or reduce what happened here to a principle of practice as in: "Start your year asking students what they might like to do in your class."

Not that this invitation isn't worthy, but this class and our turning point is more than a homily. It's grounded in a particular time and place, a particular moment of resistance, and a generational attitude. It's a moment marked when, several years after graduation, a few students came back to say hello, to tour the halls and maybe relive days gone by.

When they popped in, taking me by surprise, their first reminiscence with all the wide-eyed laughter again was recalling the *Cocktail* week of viewing.

"Hey, remember when you showed *Cocktail*? That was fresh."

Cocktail as literary canon. That's a *through line*.

THE TEACHER AS RELUCTANT WRITER

One year at an annual meeting of the National Writing Project, Kim Stafford, then director of the Lewis and Clark Writing Project in Portland, Oregon, was the keynote speaker. Stafford started by telling us he was going to ask us to write.

In all confession, I am ashamed to say this, but I just wasn't in the mood and felt rather cynical about the whole request that we write. He was serious, though, asking us to take out our notebooks then and there.

"I'm going to ask us to write today. I'm going to ask us to write about ordinary things, everyday things, and no one is going to be a prophet. The wind is a prophet. The student sitting in the back of the classroom with the sunglasses on is a prophet. But nobody here today is going to be a prophet. Today we're going to write about ordinary things, everyday things."

Stafford went on to read a few lines from "Things I Learned Last Week," a poem his father, the acclaimed poet, William Stafford, had composed. In the poem, William Stafford cites little everyday noticings that somehow, through their simplicity, seem profound, as in how "ants, when they meet each other, / usually pass on the right" (2014, p. 83).

Following the reading of his father's poem, Stafford repeated his mantra, asking us to settle into the ordinary, cautioning against any "prophetizing," all of which put me into a kind of spell, and I had no choice but to get something going.

Whatever inspired me to begin with a memory of an old college roommate, I will never know. My roommate was anything but ordinary, but I went with it, focusing on that stained army jacket she always wore. Right in the middle of my newfound thrill, however, the keynote and our time for writing came to an abrupt end, replaced by a short ceremony honoring an NWP colleague, cheating us of our deep dives into the everyday.

Then we adjourned, off to other workshops, and that was that.

Later, I ran into a colleague, and we eagerly exchanged details about the respective sessions we had just attended.

"I continued with Stafford," she offered breathlessly.

"*What?* What did he do? Did he continue with what he started with the keynote? I'm still writing my piece in my head."

As it turned out, Stafford's workshop participants continued with poetry, and as a finale, each writer reading a poem aloud. With the last reading—which, according to my colleague, turned out to be particularly stunning—Kim took a breath, turned to everyone, and asked:

"So what does this make us want to do with our lives?"

Though I was hearing this account secondhand, I knew in that moment that suggesting such a question was also something profound. In fact, I found I wanted to guard that question so it might be used sparingly (even sacredly) one day in a classroom of my own, at just the right time when it might make sense to do so. When some student might write something that stunned us and made the room silent, and I might turn to the class and say,

"So what does this poem or story or essay make us want to do with our lives?" In short, the power of writing—*literature*— moves us.

I worried that some English teacher in Kim's workshop would be as struck by Kim's delicate wisdom as I was just then and make his words into a poster overhanging the chalkboard: "So what does literature make us want to do with our lives?" I pledged I would protect that question forever as something priceless and remarkable, rescuing it from banality.

The extraordinariness of that line comes only when we recognize ordinariness in a new way. Like the taste of a pizza.

That's a breakthrough and a through line.

A STUDENT WRITER YOU NEVER FORGET

After he went away to an Ivy League university, one superior student writer contacted me to advise me to stop singling out best writers in class, suggesting how good they are, using their papers as models in class. It was painful for him to tell me how he had become very blocked, thinking he had to live up to a reputation he couldn't sustain.

Note to self: Be careful with that *accidental literary canon* you're boasting about.

LIVING WITH WHAT I'VE LEFT OUT, OR BACK TO JANET MALCOLM

First published in *The New Yorker* magazine in 1994, Malcolm's essay, "Forty-one False Starts" includes a byline underneath the title:

How does the painter David Salle know when to stop? How does the author know where to start? It's all a question of process.

Give me more room, and I could keep painting. Oh to tell "The Best Indefinite Pronoun Lesson Ever" or "Literary Mash-ups in Shanghai."

Breakthrough.

It wouldn't have mattered. The stories I drifted into, the ones that first came to mind, are sufficient in getting me somewhere just in the telling of them, however momentary.

Momentary, because even though I know these stories well, each time I bring them to mind and write about them, the rendering seems always for the first time and comes out a little differently. The angle of vision shifts.

With this writing, with these unfoldings in this moment in time, my students and I *are* the text, and I am a student of my own practice.

CONCLUSION

Angles of Vision. I really owe it to myself to annotate my essay—to drop in with fresh eyes, sticky noting, questioning, hyperlinking a noteworthy article or maybe a David Salle painting. I owe it to readers, too, to keep me honest and afloat in this protean world of what it means to teach authentically, equitably, and transformatively in the year 2023.

And so, I mark up the text. A few notations are feel-good marks that reference discoveries that may stand the test of time, that may hit a chord with other teachers and their instructional styles or serve as guideposts for newer teacher generations. Other remarks suggest I may have romanticized my practice. It's a healthy trip back.

In rereading I am struck by how my view of student writing and student commentary as part of an "accidental literary canon" is really an accidental discovery. I don't think I fully realized the extent to which student text and the ways in which students talk about each other's texts moved and centered my teaching. It was if we all are engrossed in a good book. Once students break loose of rule-driven conceptions of good writing, they take off with discovering themselves as *content creators*, detailing common ideas in extraordinary ways, or as content curators, coinventing a new curriculum.

Scholars Antero Garcia and Ernest Morrell (2022) might call this kind of teacher presence and instructional impact a matter of "tuned-in teaching."

Yet, as I pat myself on the back, the elephant on the page rears its head. Garcia and Morrell (2022) ask, "When considering what is *tuned-in* about your practice, question *for whom* and *for why*" (p. 71). In fact, where might I be *out of touch*?

With this caution, my annotations turn to regrets—regrets representative of a kind of vigilance to cultivate. I regret portraying everyday or ordinary experiences as safe spaces. Who am I leaving out when I suggest it's a simple thing to write about everydayness? What trauma might be lurking inside that request? And what of the writer who courageously writes about a debilitating shyness? What did this writer's experience listening to us take apart her text *make her want to do with her life*? Did we leave the writer behind?

Annotations such as these, some triumphant, some lamenting, should not be documented in isolation as I have done here. Going forward, I welcome the kind of public act, or "social scholarship of teaching," described by scholars Kalir and Garcia (2021) in *Annotation* where educators are encouraged "to share knowledge together and produce new meaning about teaching through the annotation of academic literature" (pp. 106–107).

Academic literature surely includes the stories we tell formally and informally about our practice. In that vein, if readers are so inclined, please go at it with my teaching and annotate away: link me to new ways of thinking; post an illuminating meme. Join me in stitching together a whole new kind of text, which, if we're on track, will be a satisfying breakthrough.

RECOMMENDED READING

Garcia, A., & Morrell, E. (2022). *Tuned-in teaching: Centering youth culture for an active and just classroom.* Heinemann. https://www.heinemann.com/products/e13647.aspx

> Part of the Not This But That series likened to the diet craze, "Eat This, Not That," this book puts readers in dialogue with Antero Garcia and Ernest Morell as they talk practitioner-to-practitioner about what makes for more connected teaching and naming what it is we need to change. Alongside a vision of tuned-in practice, they cite research that explains why some practices are outdated and what it may take to transform education for new generations of teachers and students.

Kalir, R. H., & Garcia, A. (2021). *Annotation.* The MIT Press. https://mitpress.mit.edu/9780262539920/annotation/

> This little book provides a short history of annotation as a genre, expanding notions of how annotative acts—from the markings of medieval manuscripts to the myriad digital and multimodal practices of the present—reshape what we mean by and how we interpret "text."

CHAPTER 13

Conclusion

Sandra Murphy and Mary Ann Smith

When Challenge Brings Change: How Teacher Breakthroughs Transform the Classroom explores teaching as a human endeavor, with stories and reflections that take us on the breakthrough journeys of 11 veteran teachers. According to author Parker Palmer, "Unlike many professions, teaching is always done at the dangerous intersection of personal and public life" (2017, p. 18). This collection illustrates what it means to connect all the corners in this challenging intersection—us, our students, our subjects, and the outside world.

Here, then, are some of the challenges the teacher authors faced that led them to seek a breakthrough, challenges you may recognize in your own teaching world:

- *The challenge from within*: Who we are and how our personal identity can positively contribute to the classroom. "I am my own greatest challenge," one author told us. "I learned from writing this piece that I have to be willing to experiment and change. I have to be willing to get up and start over again."
- *The challenge posed by who our students are*: How we can include and uplift every one of them with supportive relationships and meaningful learning. "We've been entrusted with the future," one of the authors explained. "If you aren't feeling the weight of it, you aren't taking the risks."
- *The challenge from outside circumstances*: Even without a pandemic—the crisis that some authors wrote about—every teacher at every grade level has to deal with school/classroom policies and politics from the outside that shape or impede learning and are ubiquitous.
- *The challenge of trading the tried-and-true for the unknown*: All the authors here have made a leap of faith in order to create something better for their students. There are no guarantees, no certainties when it comes to teaching. Teachers have to push the possibility button with or without a green light.
- *The challenge of technology*: Technology has both isolated us and brought us together in its exciting, messy, clumsy, sometimes frightening way. It has wracked our nervous systems as we've

scrambled to paste live classroom methods and materials into online platforms. And there is much more to come as artificial intelligence enters uninvited into our classrooms with its ever-expanding reach. Yet, teachers, such as the ones featured here, have set their sights on making technology in academic settings a positive force in their students' learning.

BREAKTHROUGHS LEAD TO THROUGHLINES

In our opening chapter, we discussed the variety of breakthroughs you would come across from our 11 authors and some of the key themes that might cross over from story to story—throughlines, Rebekah Caplan called them in her chapter. We also noted that breakthroughs as presented here aren't necessarily about some new practice—although some new practices appear, especially in relation to breaking rules and taking risks. Similarly, the breakthroughs here do not represent some evolving theory—for example, student-centered instruction with its specific research-based dimensions. That said, the insights of our authors lead to principles—or, call them throughlines—that will likely influence/guide their future practice, such as, being who we are in the classroom; using our life experiences to help our students; embracing risk and trial and error; trusting our ability to come up with a better way, even if we experience a few setbacks.

In addition, there are some throughlines that are, we think, qualifiers for even having a breakthrough. *Empathy* is one. Meyers et al. (2019) cite evidence that teacher empathy is one of "the strongest predictors of positive student outcomes" (p. 162). You may have noted from the breakthroughs in this collection that when teachers become the students—learning a new language, navigating their own struggles with writing, figuring out how to run a class online— they are stepping into the shoes of a learner, facing some of the challenges their students face.

In the same way, it takes *courage* to have a breakthrough. When teachers put students in the driver's seat without knowing exactly what will happen, they must rely on confidence in their students and in their mutual abilities to work the kinks out together. As one of our authors told us, "I have learned to accept that I don't have to know it all." In this collection, courage means diving into participatory online opportunities, giving students new roles as historians, infusing joy into the rigors of college learning, and sharing what's close to home with students.

And finally, the authors here exhibit the kind of *openness* that leads to discovery and transformation. They are willing to question their assumptions, approaches, roles, and relationships with their students, even at the toughest moments when schools shut down or assignments fall apart, or discomfort closes in.

THE POWER OF WRITING ABOUT CHALLENGES AND BREAKTHROUGHS

When we began the breakthroughs project, we wanted to encourage teachers to write about their classroom lives, and in doing so, revisit a challenge that led to some kind of breakthrough. We were testing the ever-expanding possibilities of writing and its role in giving writers new insights.

In the first draft of his chapter, John Levine came to a dismal conclusion, telling the reader—and himself—that inviting his first-year students to uncover their reasons for being in college was probably not a good thing. End of story. But as we imagined it would, his writing did its magic. It made him curious. Was he just assuming that his students were somehow being manipulated or damaged by questioning their education goals? Why not ask them? So he tracked down four students to find out where they landed and in what ways, if any, his reading and writing assignments might have taken them off course. Writing about his breakthrough, then, gave him a front-row seat from which to view his teaching and to craft a new ending.

When Rebekah Caplan drafted the interconnected breakthrough moments in her teaching career, she made what she calls "an accidental discovery." She had not noticed that when she used student writing as literary texts, she was creating—accidentally—a new kind of literary canon. "I never realized" she wrote, "how my full attention with student writing . . . moved and centered my teaching." The breakthrough writing did it again! Plus it gave Caplan principles or throughlines to inform her teaching in the future.

Perhaps Lisa Orta's writing experience will ring bells with some of our readers. Orta had been waiting for an excuse, or better yet, a motivator, to pour out a story she had been very eager to tell. As she recounted the moment when her community college shut down and she was enlisted in the fast and furious effort to retool an entire faculty for online teaching, she was also able to pour out the truths that will stay with her and her colleagues long after the year of crisis ended.

We hope this collection will be your motivation to write about your own challenges and breakthroughs—to discover and rediscover what is true about your teaching life. Parker Palmer reminds us, "The more familiar we are with our inner terrain, the more sure-footed our teaching—and living—becomes" (Palmer, 2017, p. 6). We encourage you to roam your practice and mine it for indelible breakthroughs, for throughlines that embody what you know and value and want to share.

> The most exciting breakthroughs of the 21st century will not occur because of technology but because of an expanding concept of what it means to be human.
>
> —Naisbitt & Aburdene, 1990, p. 16

References

Ahmad, F. (2019, January 30). A letter to multilingual students. *The Cornell Sun.* https://cornellsun.com/2019/01/30/ahmad-a-letter-to-multilingual-students/

Ahonen, P., Blomberg, A., Doerr, K., Einola, K., Elkina, A., Gao, G., Hambleton, J., Helin, J., Huopalainen, A., Johannsen, B. F., Johansson, J., Jääskeläinen, P., Kaasila-Pakanen, A. L., Kivinen, N., Mandalaki, E., Meriläinen, S., Pullen, A., Salmela, T., Satama, S., . . . Zhang, L. E. (2020). Writing resistance together. *Gender, Work, & Organization, 27*(4), 447–470.

Albers, C. (1942). A young evacuee of Japanese ancestry waits with the family baggage before leaving for an assembly center. [Photograph]. https://commons.wikimedia.org/wiki/File:A_young_evacuee_of_Japanese_ancestry_waits_with_the_family_baggage_before_leaving_by_bus_for_an_assembly_center..._-_NARA_-_539959.jpg

Andelora, J. (2008). Forging a national identity: TYCA and the two-year college teacher-scholar. *Teaching English in the Two-Year College, 35*(4), 350–362.

Baez, J., Marquart, M. S., Garay, K., & Chung, R. (2020). Trauma-informed teaching and learning online: Principles & practices during a global health crisis. Columbia University Libraries. https://academiccommons.columbia.edu/doi/10.7916/d8-gc9d-na95

Banks, J. A. (1993). The canon debate, knowledge construction, and multicultural education. *Educational Researcher, 22*(5), 4–14. https://doi.org/10.3102/0013189X022005004

Bartholomae, D. (1985). Inventing the university. In M. Rose (Ed.), *When writers can't write* (pp. 134–165). The Guilford Press.

Bauman, A., & Peterson, A. (Eds.). (2002). *Breakthroughs: Classroom discoveries about teaching writing.* National Writing Project.

Bem, S., & Lewis, S. A. (1975). Sex role adaptability: One consequence of psychological androgyny. *Journal of Personality and Social Psychology, 31*(4), 634–643. https://psycnet.apa.org/record/1975-31771-001

Bonnello, C. (2019). *Underdogs.* Unbound Digital.

Britton, E. R., & Leonard, R. L. (2020). The social justice potential of critical reflection and critical language awareness pedagogies for L2 writers. *Journal of Second Language Writing, 50.* https://doi.org/10.1016/j.jslw.2020.100776

Britton, J. (1970). *Language and learning.* Penguin.

Buchholz, B. A., DeHart, J., & Moorman, G. (2020). Digital citizenship during a global pandemic: Moving beyond digital literacy. *Journal of Adolescent & Adult Literacy, 64*(1), 11–17. https://doi.org/10.1002/jaal.1076

Butler, J. (1999). *Gender trouble: Feminism and the subversion of identity*. Routledge.

California Community Colleges Key Facts. (2023). California Community Colleges. https://www.cccco.edu/About-Us/Key-Facts

Cameron, J. (2016). *The artist's way*. TarcherPerigee.

Caplan, B. (2018, January). The world might be better off without college for everyone. *The Atlantic*. https://www.theatlantic.com/magazine/archive/2018/01/whats-college-good-for/546590/

Caplan, R. (1984). *Writers in training*. Dale Seymour Publications. https://www.amazon.com/Writers-Training-Rebekah-Caplan/dp/0866512039

Carwil-Bjork, J. (2021). New maps for an inclusive Wikipedia: Decolonial scholarship and strategies to counter systemic bias. *New Review of Hypermedia and Multimedia, 27*(3), 207–228. https://doi.org/10.1080/13614568.2020.1865463

Chong, P. (2013). *Undesirable elements: Real people, real lives, real theater*. Theatre Communications Group Inc.

Collaboration, Diversity, and Inclusion Supplement. (2021, June 25). *Wikimedia, Meta-Wiki*. https://meta.wikimedia.org/wiki/Community_Insights/Community_Insights_2021_Report/Collaboration,_Diversity_%26_Inclusion_(2021)

Community and Newcomer Diversity. (2021, December 10). *Community Insights 2021 Report. Wikimedia Meta-Wiki*. https://meta.wikimedia.org/wiki/Community_Insights/Community_Insights_2021_Report/Thriving_Movement#Community_and_Newcomer_Diversity

Conference on College Composition and Communication. (2020, May). CCCC *statement on second language writing and multilingual writers*. https://cccc.ncte.org/cccc/resources/positions/secondlangwriting

Cook, J. M. (2021, April 30). Students bring indigenous perspectives to Wikipedia. *Folio*. https://www.ualberta.ca/folio/2021/04/students-bring-indigenous-perspectives-to-wikipedia.html

Countee Cullen: Revision History. (2023, May 30). https://en.wikipedia.org/w/index.php?title=Countee_Cullen&action=history

Cox, R. D. (2009). *The college fear factor: How students and professors misunderstand one another*. Harvard University Press.

Cruz, C. (2012, September). Author talk. *The Chabot Puente Project's Chicanx/Latinx Heritage Month Speaker Series*. Chabot College, Hayward, CA, United States.

Cullen, C. (1925, March 1). Heritage. *The Survey Graphic. 53*(11). 674-675. https://umedia.lib.umn.edu/item/p16022coll336:2133/p16022coll336:2081?child_index=52&query=&sidebar_page=18

Cummings, R. E. (2020). Writing knowledge: Wikipedia, public review, and peer review. *Studies in Higher Education, 45*(5), 950–962. https://doi.org/10.1080/03075079.2020.1749791

Daley-Ward, Y. (2021). *The how: Notes on the great work of meeting yourself*. Penguin Books.

Dana, N. (2002). Teacher inquiry defined. https://www.sagepub.com/sites/default/files/upm-binaries/7119_dana_ch_1.pdf

Davidson, S. (2017). Trauma-informed practices for a postsecondary education: A guide. *Education Northwest*. https://educationnorthwest.org/sites/default/files/resources/trauma-informed-practices-postsecondary-508.pdf

Davis, A. P. (2023, May 30). https://en.wikipedia.org/wiki/Arthur_P._Davis

Dawson, C. M. (2017). *The teacher-writer: Creating writing groups for personal and professional growth*. Teachers College Press.

De Castella, K., Byrne, D., & Covington, M. (2013). Unmotivated or motivated to fail? A cross-cultural study of achievement motivation, fear of failure, and student disengagement. *Journal of Educational Psychology, 105*(3), 861–880.

Dennis-Tiwary, T. (2022). *Future tense: Why anxiety is good for you (even though it feels bad)*. Piatkus.

Deresiewicz, W. (2015). *Excellent sheep: The miseducation of the American elite and the way to a meaningful life*. Free Press.

Diamond, C. T. (1993). Writing to reclaim self: The use of narrative in teacher education. *Teaching & Teacher Education, 9*(5/6), 511–517.

Diaz, J. (1996). How to date a brown girl. *Drown* (pp. 143–149). Riverhead Books.

Du Bois, W. E. B. (2023, January 24). *The Crisis: Journal of the National Association for the Advancement of Colored People*. https://en.wikipedia.org/wiki/The_Crisis

Dweck, C. (2006). *Mindset: The new psychology of success*. Random House.

Elbow, P. (1986). *Embracing contraries: Explorations in learning and teaching*. Oxford University Press.

Emig, J. (1977). Writing as a mode of learning. *College Composition and Communication, 28*(2), 122–128.

Episode 81: Cheryl Hogue Smith. (2021, September 15). *Pedagogue*. https://www.pedagoguepodcast.com/episodes.html

Ershler, A. R. (2001). The narrative as an experience text: Writing themselves back in. In A. Lieberman & L. Miller (Eds.), *Teachers caught in the action: Professional development that matters* (pp. 159–173). Teachers College Press.

Esslin, M. (1999, January 22). Jacques Lecoq obituary. *The Guardian*. https://www.theguardian.com/news/1999/jan/23/guardianobituaries

Fitzgerald, F. S. (2004). *The great Gatsby*. Simon & Schuster. (Originally published April 10, 1925).

Flanagan, N. (2020). *Nora Flanagan: What COVID-19 revealed about US schools—and 4 ways to rethink education* [Video]. TED Conferences. https://www.ted.com/talks/nora_flanagan_what_covid_19_revealed_about_us_schools_and_4_ways_to_rethink_education

Forbes, L. (2021). The process of play in learning in higher education: A phenomenological study. *Journal of Teaching and Learning, 15*(1), 57–73. https://.doi.org/10.22329/jtl.v15i1.6515

Foucault, M. (1980). *The history of sexuality, vol. 1: An introduction*. Vintage Books.

Fremont High School Students. (2022, September 1). What grown-ups don't understand about school. *The New York Times*. https://www.nytimes.com/2022/09/01/opinion/us-high-school-oakland.Html

Garcia, A., & Morrell, E. (2022). *Tuned-in teaching: Centering youth culture for an active and just classroom*. Heinemann.

Gebhard, N. (2015, August 2). Four steps to choosing a college major. *New York Times*. https://www.nytimes.com/2015/08/02/education/edlife/four-steps-to-choosing-a-career-path.html

Gonzalez, J. (2021, May 16). No more easy button: A suggested approach to post-pandemic teaching. *Cult of Pedagogy.* https://www.cultofpedagogy.com/easy-button/

Hammond, Z. (2015). *Culturally responsive teaching and the brain: Promoting authentic engagement and rigor among culturally and linguistically diverse students.* Corwin.

Hargreaves, A. (2022, November 18). *The disengaged generation: Improving student engagement and wellbeing in schools.* [Conference presentation]. Teaching struggling brains: Improving mental health, focus, motivation, and learning in a distressed, digital generation. Boston, MA, United States.

Harlem Renaissance. (2022, December 24). https://en.wikipedia.org/w/index.php?title=Harlem_Renaissance&oldid=1129302749

Hernandez, E. (1982). Sun mad raisins. *Art in Print.* https://artinprint.org/article/ester-hernandez-sun-mad/

hooks, b. (2001). *All about love: New visions* (pp. 1–13, 45–49). Harper Collins.

hooks, b. (2003). *Teaching community: A pedagogy of hope* (pp. 127–137). Routledge.

hooks, b. (2010). *Teaching critical thinking: Practical wisdom.* Routledge.

Hoagland, T. (2010). Personal. *Unincorporated persons in the late Honda dynasty.* Graywolf Press.

Ignore All Rules. (2023, May 30). https://en.wikipedia.org/w/index.php?title=Ignore_all_rules&oldid=1153766481

Inoue, A. (2015). *Antiracist writing assessment ecologies: Teaching and assessing writing for a socially just future.* Parlor Press.

"I Wish I'd Been There." (1984). *American Heritage, 36*(1).

Jensen, D., Calhoon-Dillahunt, C., Griffiths, B., & Toth, C. (2021). Embracing the democratic promise: Transforming two-year colleges and writing studies through professional engagement. *New Directions for Community Colleges, 55–66.*

Johnson, G. D. (2023, January 11). https://en.wikipedia.org/wiki/Georgia_Douglas_Johnson

Jones, J. (2021). LGBT identification rises to 5.6% in latest U.S. estimate. *Gallup.* https://news.gallup.com/poll/329708/lgbt-identification-rises-latest-estimate.aspx

Kalir, R. H., & Garcia, A. (2021). *Annotation.* The MIT Press. https://mitpress.mit.edu/9780262539920/annotation/

Kars, M. (1997). History in a grain of sand: Teaching the historian's craft. *The Journal of American History, 83*(4), 1340. https://doi.org/10.2307/2952905

Kelin, D. A. (2009). *In their own words: Drama with young English language learners.* New Plays Books.

Key & Peele. [Comedy Central] (2015, July 28). Teaching Center. You Tube. https://youtu.be/dkHqPFbxmOU

Kingsley A., & Orta, L. (2022, March 23). *Lifelines: Layered voices in the pivot to online instruction* [Faculty Lecture]. https://www.dvc.edu/about/governance/faculty-senate/lifelines.html

Kiriakos, C. M., & Tienari, J. (2018). Academic writing as love. *Management Learning, 49*(3), 262–277.

Kobabe, M. (2019). *Gender queer.* Oni Press.

Kornfeld, J., & Goodman, J. (1998). Melting the glaze: Exploring student responses to liberatory social studies. *Theory Into Practice, 37*(4), 306–313. https://www .jstor.org/stable/1477264

Lahiri, J. (2015, December 7). Teach yourself Italian. *The New Yorker.* https://www .newyorker.com/magazine/2015/12/07/teach-yourself-italian

Larson, H. (2018). Epistemic authority in composition studies: Tenuous relationship between two-year college faculty and knowledge production. *Teaching English in the Two-Year College, 46*(2), 109–136.

Leu, D. J., & Kinzer, C. K. (2000). The convergence of literacy instruction with networked technologies for information and communication. *Reading Research Quarterly, 35*(1), 108–112. https://doi.org/10.1598/RRQ.35.1.8

Lévesque, S. (2009). *Thinking historically: Educating students for the twenty-first century.* University of Toronto Press.

Levine, L. W. (1989). *The historian and the icon: Photography and the history of the American People in the 1930s and 1940s, Documenting America, 1935–1943.* University of California Press. https://nationalhumanitiescenter.org/ows /seminars/tcentury/fsaphotos/levine.pdf

Lindneux, R. (1942). *Trail of tears* [Painting], PBS. https://www.pbs.org/wgbh/aia /part4/4h1567.html

Loewen, J. (1995). Introduction to lies my teacher told me. *History and Social Justice.* https://justice.tougaloo.edu/truth/k-12/resources/introduction-to-lies-my -teacher-told-me/

Lugosi, N. V., Patrie, N., & Cromwell, K. (2022). Theorizing and implementing meaningful Indigenization: Wikipedia as an opportunity for course-based digital advocacy. *Critical Studies in Education*, 1–17. https://doi.org/10.1080/175 08487.2022.2074489

Malcolm, J. (2014). Forty-one false starts. *The New Yorker.* https://www.newyorker .com/magazine/1994/07/11/forty-one-false-starts

Malcolm, J. (2013). *Forty-one false starts: Essays on artists and writers.* Farrar, Straus and Giroux. https://us.macmillan.com/fsg/?q=forty-one%20false%20starts

Mansharamani, V. (2022, June 15). Harvard lecturer: 'No specific skill will get you ahead in the future'—but this 'way of thinking' will. https://www.cnbc .com/2020/06/15/harvard-yale-researcher-future-success-is-not-a-specific-skill -its-a-type-of-thinking.html

Markham, R. H. & Waddell, M. L. (1971). *10 steps in writing the research paper.* Barron's Educational Series.

Martinez, A. Y. (2020). *Counterstory: The rhetoric and writing of critical race theory.* NCTE.

Matsuda, P. K. (2012). Let's face it: Language issues and the writing program administrator. *WPA: Writing Program Administration, 36*(1), 141–163.

Matsuda, P. K., & Cox, M. (2011). Reading an ESL writer's text. *Studies in Self-Access Learning Journal, 2*(1), 4–14. https://sisaljournal.org/archives/mar11 /matsuda_cox/

Maung, R. (2021, May 14). Figure 3.3 and 3.4. Retrieved from Community Insights Report. *Wikimedia, MetaWiki.* https://meta.wikimedia.org/wiki/Community _Insights/Community_Insights_2021_Report/Thriving_Movement#Community _and_Newcomer_Diversity

Mezirow, J. (1991). *Transformative dimensions of adult learning.* Wiley.

Milenkova, V., & Lendzhova, V. (2021). Digital citizenship and digital literacy in the conditions of social crisis. *Computers, 10*(4), 40. https://doi.org/10.3390/computers10040040

Miles, T. (2021). *All that she carried: The journey of Ashley's sack, a Black family keepsake.* Random House.

Montez, N. (2017). Decolonizing Wikipedia through advocacy and activism: The Latina/o Theatre Wikiturgy Project. *Theatre Topics, 27*(1), E-1. https://doi.org/10.1353/tt.2017.0012

Motha, S. (2014). *Race, empire, and English language teaching.* Teachers College Press.

Muhammad, G. (2023). *Unearthing joy: A guide to culturally and historically responsive curriculum and instruction.* Scholastic.

Nagoski, E., & Nagoski, A. (2020). Joyfully ever after. In *Burnout: The secret to unlocking the stress cycle* (pp. 213–215). Ballantine Books.

Naisbitt, J., & Aburdene P. (1990). *Megatrends 2000: Ten new directions for the 1990's.* William Morrow and Company, Inc.

Nemi Neto, J. (2018). Queer pedagogy: Approaches to inclusive teaching. *Policy Futures in Education, 16*(5), 589–604. https://doi.org/10.1177/1478210317751273

Nieto, S. (2006). Solidarity, courage and heart: what teacher educators can learn from a new generation of teachers. *Intercultural Education, 17*(5), 457–473.

Ofgang, E. (2021, September 9). 4 lessons from remote learning. *Tech & Learning.* https://www.techlearning.com/how-to/4-lessons-from-remote-learning

Palmer, P. J. (2017). *The courage to teach.* Jossey-Bass.

Passing (novel): Revision history. (2023, January 16). https://en.wikipedia.org/wiki/Passing_(novel)

Phillips, C., & Giordano, J. B. (2020). Messy processes into and out of failure: Professional identities and open-access writers. In A. D. Carr & L. R. Micciche (Eds.), *Failure pedagogies: Learning and unlearning what it means to fail* (pp. 153–162). Peter Lang Publishing.

Purdy, J. P. (2009). When the tenets of composition go public: A study of writing in Wikipedia. *College Composition and Communication, 61*(2), W351. https://www.academia.edu/8613597/When_the_Tenets_of_Composition_Go_Public_A_Study_of_Writing_in_Wikipedia

Purdy, J. P. (2020). A decade of writing on Wikipedia. *First Monday.* https://doi.org/10.5210/fm.v25i9.10857

Ray, B. (2019, October 21). How to help young people transition into adulthood. *Greater Good.* https://greatergood.berkeley.edu/article/item/how_to_help_young_people_transition_into_adulthood

Reading, Writing and Researching the Harlem Renaissance (Fall 2013). WikiEdu. https://dashboard.wikiedu.org/

Rose, M. (1989). *Lives on the boundary: The struggles and achievements of America's underprepared.* The Free Press.

Saidy, C. (2018). Beyond words on the page: Using multimodal composing to aid in the transition to first-year writing. *Teaching English in the Two-Year College, 45*(3), 255–273.

Schwartz, S. (2022, August 11). Who decides what history we teach? An explainer. *Education Week.* https://www.edweek.org/teaching-learning/who-decides-what -history-we-teach-an-explainer/2021/08

Shaughnessy, M. (1977). *Errors and expectations: A guide for the teacher of basic writing.* Oxford University Press.

Smith, A. (2015). *Conquest: Sexual violence and American Indian genocide.* Duke University Press.

Smith, C. H. (2012). Interrogating texts: From deferent to efferent and aesthetic reading practices. *Journal of Basic Writing, 31*(1), 59–79.

Smith, C. H. (2013). Postcards from the beach. *California English, 19*(1), 26–27.

Smith, C. H. (2019). "All truly great thoughts are conceived while walking": Academic inclusion through multimodal walkabouts. *Teaching English in the Two-Year College, 47*(1), 18–21.

Sommers, N. (1980). Revision strategies of student writers and experienced adult writers. *College Composition and Communication, 31*(4), 378–388. https:// www.jstor.org/stable/356588

Sommers, N. (2013). *Responding to student writers.* Macmillan.

Stafford, W. (2014). Things I learned last week. In *Ask me: 100 essential poems of William Stafford.* Graywolf Press. https://www.graywolfpress.org/books/ask-me

Stephens, A. (n.d.). Transgender Americans belong: An open letter to America's employers. *Out & Equal.* https://outandequal.org/aimee-stephens-letter-to-employers/

Stewart, B. & Ju, B.(2020). On Black Wikipedians: Motivations behind content contribution. *Information Processing & Management, 57*(3), https://doi.org /10.1016/j.ipm.2019.102134

Sullivan, P. (2015a). The two-year college teacher-scholar-activist. *Teaching English in the Two-Year College, 42*(4), 327–350.

Sullivan, P. (2015b). The UnEssay: Making room for creativity in the composition classroom. *College Composition and Communication, 67*(1), 6–34.

Swain, M. (2013). The inseparability of cognition and emotion in second language learning. *Language Teaching, 46*(2), 195–207.

The New London Group. (1996). A pedagogy of multiliteracies. *Harvard Educational Review, 66*(1), 60–92.

Thompson, M. (2020, December 9). Are we teaching in a new world?: Yahdon Israel on language barriers, educational politics, and online teaching. *Teachers & Writers Magazine.* https://teachersandwritersmagazine.org/are-we-teaching -in-a-new-world-yahdon-israel-on-language-barriers-educational-politics-and -online-teaching/

Tomaš, Z., & Shapiro, S. (2021). From crisis to opportunity: Turning questions about "plagiarism" into conversations about linguistically responsive pedagogy. *TESOL Quarterly, 55*(4), 1102–1113.

Toth, C., Sullivan, P., & Calhoon-Dillahunt, C. (2019). Two-year college teacher-scholar-activism: Reconstructing the disciplinary matrix of writing studies. *College Composition and Communication, 71*(1), 86–116.

Valdez, L. (1990). Los vendidos and the militants. In *Early works: Actos, Bernabe and Pensamiento Serpentino.* Arte Publico.

Vohland, K., Land-Zanstra, A., Ceccaroni, L., Lemmens, R., Perrello, J., Ponti, M. Samson, R., & Wagenknecht, K. (Eds.). (2021). *The science of citizen science.* Springer Nature. https://library.oapen.org/handle/20.500.12657/46119

Waite, S. (2017). *Teaching queer: Radical possibilities for writing and knowing.* University of Pittsburgh Press.

Walker, A. (2010). *Hard times require furious dancing.* New World Library.

Wang, W. (2017). *Chemistry: A novel.* Knopf.

Ward, J. (2018). *Sing, unburied, sing.* Scribner.

Warner, M. (1991). Introduction: Fear of a queer planet. *Social Text, 29,* 3–17. http://www.jstor.org/stable/466295

Weird etymology. (2021). *Oxford Languages and Google.* Oxford Languages. Accessed August 10, 2021, https://www.google.com/search?q=weird+etymology

Whitehead, A. N. (1929). *The aims of education and other essays.* MacMillan.

Whitney, A. (2008) Teacher transformation in the National Writing Project. *Research in the Teaching of English, 43*(2), 144–187.

Wikipedia: Five Pillars (2023, May 30). https://en.wikipedia.org/wiki /Wikipedia:Five_pillars

Wilkerson, I. (2016). The long-lasting legacy of the great migration. *Smithsonian Magazine.* https://www.smithsonianmag.com/history/long-lasting-legacy-great -migration-180960118/

Xing, J. & Vetter. (2020). Editing for equity: Understanding instructor motivations for integrating cross-disciplinary Wikipedia assignments. *First Monday.* https:// firstmonday.org/ojs/index.php/fm/article/download/10575/9552

Yancey, K. B. (2009). *Writing in the 21st century: A report from the National Council of Teachers of English.* National Council of Teachers of English. https://cdn .ncte.org/nctefiles/press/yancey_final.pdf

Yarmolinsky, A. (1954). *The unknown Chekhov: Stories and other writings hitherto untranslated.* Noonday Press.

Yoshino, K. (2007). *Covering.* Random House.

Yosso, T. (2005). Whose culture has capital? A critical race theory discussion of community cultural wealth. *Race Ethnicity and Education, 8*(1), 69–91. https:// doi.org/10.1080/1361332052000341006

Zeichner, K. M. (2005). Research on teacher thinking and different views of reflective practice in teaching and teacher education. In I. Carlagran, G. Handal, & S. Vaage (Eds.), *Teachers' minds and actions: Research on teachers' thinking and practice* (pp. 9–28). Falmer Press.

Zinsser, W. (1988). *Writing to learn.* Harper and Row.

Zoch, M., Myers, J., Lambert, C., Vetter, A., & Fairbanks, C. (2016). Reimagining instructional practices: Exploring the identity work of teachers of writing. *Teaching/Writing: The Journal of Writing Teacher Education, 5*(1), 1–23.

Index

Note: *f* denotes figure in the index below.

About the Editors and Contributors

Rebekah Caplan serves as Associate Director for Professional Development for the UC Berkeley Bay Area Writing Project, where she coordinates professional development programs for school districts requesting workshops on the teaching and learning of writing. A veteran high school teacher, Rebekah has recently taught summer academic writing courses for high school students in Shanghai, China, and at the American School of Kuwait in collaboration with the Center for the Professional Education of Teachers, Teachers College at Columbia University. Prior to her current leadership role with the Bay Area Writing Project, Rebekah served as a literacy specialist for the National Center on Education and the Economy where she led literacy workshops nationally and developed curriculum materials for schools seeking guidance in standards-based reforms in the teaching of writing.

Kelly Crosby has been a lecturer in the UC Davis University Writing Program (UWP) since 2013. She began her career as an adult literacy/GED teacher, then moved on to teaching high school ESL in Fairfax County, Virginia. Kelly has also taught English as a Foreign Language in Brazil, high school Spanish and ELD in Sacramento, California, and many areas of intensive English at UC Davis Continuing Education. In the University Writing Program, she teaches first-year writing for English learners, professional writing for prospective teachers, and coordinates a K–12 literacy support internship program. Kelly became a teacher consultant with the Area 3 Writing Project in 2020 and is grateful for the enduring K–16 teacher connections built at writing project sites.

Beth Daly is an English, drama, and ELD teacher at San Lorenzo High School in California. She received a BFA in drama from California Institute of the Arts and an MA in education from UC Berkeley. She served as a Peace Corps English education volunteer in Moldova from 2015–2017. As the drama teacher at San Lorenzo High School, Beth has directed numerous productions including *The Laramie Project, The House on Mango Street, In and Out of Shadows,* student-written adaptations of *Our Town* and *Much Ado about Nothing,* and a student-created documentary theater piece titled *The Russell City Project.* She has been a teacher consultant with the Bay

Area Writing Project (BAWP) since 2010, and she has taught in BAWP's young writers camps in the Bay Area and in China.

Anne Kingsley is a Professor of English at Diablo Valley College. She is interested in the ways technology and digital platforms can be used creatively in the writing and literature classroom. She began her teaching career in 2002, serving students in a non-profit organization, Friends of Island Academy, that works with formerly incarcerated and justice impacted youth. She taught in literacy, Pre GED, and GED classrooms. This work was foundational in her pursuit of social justice and education, and her students remain inspirational to any work she performs today. She is grateful for opportunities to connect with and share student voices.

Kristin Land has taught English composition and literature, as well as creative writing, in Hayward, California, since 2001. She began her career at Tennyson High School before transitioning to Chabot Community College in 2010. She strives to design and implement transformative, trauma-informed learning experiences rooted in social justice, and she is grateful for professional collaborations that support such work, especially for her colleagues in the Puente Project, the Change It Now Learning Community, and the Bay Area Writing Project. (She was BAWPtized, as they say, in 2005.) In 2014, guided by BAWP principles and the visionary leadership of Carmen Johnston, Kristin co-founded The Chabot Collaborative for Equity and Professional Growth, a college-based center for teaching and learning that invites classified professionals, faculty, and administrators to hold one another ever more accountable for interrupting inequity. She is honored to work alongside a growing coalition of equity-minded educators who lovingly challenge one another to deepen their craft and to uplift students' linguistic and cultural assets.

John Levine teaches composition, public speaking, and creative writing at UC Berkeley, where he has been on the College Writing Programs faculty for more than 20 years. He has also led numerous workshops for teachers and students through the Bay Area Writing Project. An award-winning playwright, he has had plays produced throughout the United States. International productions include India, Australia, Canada, Mexico, the Philippines, the U.A.E., and the U.K. His creative and academic work has been published in a number of anthologies. More information at johnlevineplaywright.com

Sandra Murphy, formerly a high school teacher of English and journalism, is now professor emerita at the University of California, Davis, where she acted as faculty advisor to the Area 3 Writing Project. She served on the Standing Committee for the National Assessment of Educational Progress and co-authored the Common Core State Standards for writing. Among her publications are three she has written with her co-editor of this volume, Mary Ann Smith: *Writing Portfolios: A Bridge from Teaching to Assessment, Uncommonly Good Ideas: Teaching Writing in the Common Core Era, and Writing to Make an Impact.* Her most recent publication is *Assessing Writing to Support Learning: Turning Accountability Inside Out* (with Peggy O'Neill). According to Sandra, what she knows about teaching writing is anchored in her experience as a teacher and in what she has learned from the many talented teachers and researchers she has worked with over the years.

Lisa Orta participated in the Bay Area Writing Project Institute at UC Berkeley in the summer of 1990, while teaching English at Skyline High School in Oakland, California, and being pregnant with her first child. She and her baby attended a National Writing Project Institute at Princeton in the summer of 1991. She joined the Diablo Valley College English Department in Pleasant Hill, California, in 1995. In addition to her teaching assignment, she coordinated Nexus, the college's year-long new faculty orientation program, Staff Development, and taught in London for the Study Abroad program. She began working with online instruction in 2002 and is a member of the DVC Distance Education team.

Stan Pesick taught 11th grade American history and 12th grade American government/economics in the Oakland Unified School District (OUSD), 1976–1994. Between 2001 and 2011, he co-directed OUSD's History/Social Studies department. Between 2011 and 2014, he co-directed the Oakland Unified School District/Mills College History-English Language Arts (ELA) Collaborative on Writing the Argumentative Essay. Since 2014, he has worked as a curriculum consultant to the National Japanese American Historical Society and National Park Service. He recently completed work with the National Writing Project to develop instructional materials to support students' civically-engaged writing. Stan holds a PhD in Curriculum and Instruction from Stanford University.

Rob Rogers is a writer, teacher, and journalist who works with 11th- and 12th-grade students at De La Salle High School in Concord and lives in Vallejo, California. When he isn't nattering on about transcendentalism, the American Dream, or slam poetry, you can generally find him puttering in the garden with his wife, learning to play harmonica, practicing archery, or playing heroes and villains with his 9- and 12-year-old sons. He grew up in Plymouth, Massachusetts, attended Kenyon College, and spent several years as a newspaper reporter and travel writer before finding his home in the classroom. He is a strong believer in the power of stories, the need for creative self-expression and the 12-bar blues. He also likes coffee.

Cheryl Hogue Smith began her teaching career as a Lecturer at California State University, Bakersfield. She is now a Professor of English at Kingsborough Community College of the City University of New York in Brooklyn. Cheryl is also the Writing and Reading Across the Curriculum Certification Coordinator at Kingsborough. Cheryl is a past Chair of the Two-Year College English Association. She is also a Fellow of the National Writing Project (SCWriP). She has published articles in *TETYC*, *JBW*, *JAAL*, *English Journal*, *JTW*, *California English* and chapters in *What Is "College-Level" Writing?* (vol.2, NCTE), *Deep Reading, Deep Learning* (vol. 2, Peter Lang), and the forthcoming *Challenging Antisemitism: Lessons from Literacy Classrooms* (Rowman & Littlefield).

Mary Ann Smith started out as a secondary English and journalism teacher which was the foundation for all that came next. She directed the Bay Area and California Writing Projects, co-directed the National Writing Project and served as its government relations director. During this time, Mary Ann had the good fortune to work with and learn from teachers around the country and on military bases abroad. She has had numerous occasions to feature the extraordinary work that teachers do, including during invited testimonies before U.S. House and Senate subcommittees and in seven books and multiple articles. Her happiest place to be is the beach and her super power is her loving, occasionally boisterous family.

James Andrew Wilson (they/them) is an English professor at Diablo Valley College in Pleasant Hill, California. James came to community college teaching in 2013 after an errant path as a performer, writer, and seemingly eternal grad student. Now, they are proud to co-coordinate the state's first community college queer learning community, Community of Pride. Prior to teaching, they created performance work in the United States, Canada, and Europe and published articles in *Performance Studies* and *Contemporary Theatre Review*. Now, outside of grading essays, reading, prepping, and doing other campus work, they create solo performance pieces. Find out more at www.james-andrew-wilson.com.